MW01615192

SEXUAL BROKENNESS

— AND THE —
HOPE OF THE GOSPEL

EDITED BY RUSSELL MOORE

Leland House Press
The Ethics & Religious Liberty Commission
901 Commerce Street, Suite 550
Nashville, TN 37203

Leland House Press is an initiative of The Ethics & Religious Liberty Commission
(SBC) made possible by the sacrificial gifts of Southern Baptists to the Cooperative
Program. We are grateful for the Cooperative Program and the prayerful support of
Southern Baptists around the world.

ISBN-13: 978-0990906162
ISBN-10: 0990906167

PREFACE

The devil has no shortage of tools for destroying lives. And in today's culture, one of his most effective tools is a distorted view of sexuality. The wreckage of such a view is everywhere: A marriage is broken by infidelity. A child is abused by a relative. A pastor is forced from his ministry due to a pornography addiction. A college student thinks back on her one-night stand with deep regret and a wounded heart. Perhaps no other human desire has been so distorted by our culture as sex. To borrow an illustration from C. S. Lewis, sexual desire has become like a piano key that is played at all the wrong times. Though God designed it for beautiful melodies, it has instead soured the music.

But there is good news. There is hope, because the gospel of Christ has the power to bind up every broken heart and heal every wound. The Word of God tells us that Jesus died to reconcile the sexually broken to himself. At the cross, he poured out his blood to make them whole again and to purify them from every transgression. As members of Christ's church, we have been entrusted with this ministry of reconciliation, and we know that the gates of hell cannot prevail against us. We have been called by the Spirit to speak prophetically to our culture and to preach forgiveness to the sexually broken. Our goal for this book is to encourage and equip believers to fulfill that mission.

In April 2014, the Ethics & Religious Liberty Commission of the Southern Baptist Convention hosted its first annual Leadership Summit in Nashville, Tennessee. Its focus was "The Gospel and Human Sexuality." The following chapters contain several lectures and sermons that were delivered at that event. All have been slightly edited for clarity, readability, and brevity.

Russell Moore, President of the ERLC, sets the stage for the rest of the chapters by showing how issues of marriage and sexuality cannot be rightly understood without first grasping the heart of the gospel. A gospel-driven church will have the power to bring healing to sexual brokenness.

Andrew Walker then provides an overview of how American society's perception of marriage is rapidly changing. He lays out a number of threats to marriage within the broader culture and within the church.

Next, **J.D. Greear** offers advice for how pastors and Christian teachers can impart a biblical view of sexuality and counsel those who are struggling with sexual sin. He pays particular attention to how the gospel can overcome the idolatrous desires of the heart. Greear concludes with a number of helpful points for discussing the issue of same-sex marriage.

Jonathan Akin uses the book of Proverbs to provide biblical wisdom on resisting sexual temptation.

The following two chapters by **David Prince** and **Jimmy Scroggins** provide counsel to churches and to parents for equipping children with a biblical view of marriage and sexuality. They also discuss many of the dangers and temptations that today's children face and how the gospel is the only answer to sexual sin.

Heath Lambert gives an exposition of Proverbs 7 and discusses how it relates to pornography, one of the most destructive forces in our culture. He provides biblical strategies for resisting the temptations of pornography. Lambert also shares with pastors and other church leaders ways that they can fight against pornography use in their churches.

Trillia Newbell then provides a brief reflection on several issues of sexual brokenness that particularly effect women. She advises churches how they can better serve women in those areas.

Tony Merida takes on the issue of sex trafficking. He sheds light on the extent of this growing problem in the United States and around the world. In doing so, Merida provides a biblical foundation for social justice and describes several ways that individuals can join in the fight against sex trafficking.

Finally, **Kevin Smith** offers a sermon on Hebrews 13, in which he outlines several ways in which believers and churches can fulfill God's command to keep the marriage bed pure.

Several study questions are provided at the end of each

chapter. These questions are intended for personal reflection or for use in small group discussions.

Our prayer is that as you read these chapters you will renew your commitment to sexual purity and to the faithfulness of marriage and that you will be emboldened to serve those who need to hear God's truth about sexuality, both inside and outside of the church. May we in all things honor the one to whom the mystery of marriage and sexuality points—the Lord Jesus Christ.

Leland House Press
October 2014

CONTRIBUTORS

Jonathan Akin serves as Senior Pastor of Fairview Baptist Church in Lebanon, Tenn., and as an adjunct professor at The Southern Baptist Theological Seminary. He previously served as a campus pastor at Highview Baptist Church in Louisville, Ky. He completed three degrees at Southern Seminary, including a Ph.D. in Old Testament. He is married to Ashley, and they have three children.

J.D. Greear is the lead pastor of The Summit Church in Raleigh-Durham, N.C. He completed his Ph.D. in Theology at Southeastern Baptist Theological Seminary, where he is also a faculty member. He and his wife Veronica live in Raleigh, N.C., and are raising four children: Kharis, Alethia, Ryah, and Adon. He is the author of *Gospel: Recovering the Power that Made Christianity Revolutionary* (2011) and *Stop Asking Jesus into Your Heart: How to Know for Sure You Are Saved* (2013).

Heath Lambert is Executive Director of the Association of Certified Biblical Counselors and associate professor of biblical counseling at The Southern Baptist Theological Seminary and its undergraduate institution, Boyce College. He received his Ph.D. from Southern Seminary and is the author of *Finally Free: Fighting for Purity with the Power of Grace* (2013). Dr. Lambert has served in pastoral ministry at churches in Kentucky and North Carolina. He and his wife, Lauren, have three children: two sons, Carson and Connor, and a daughter, Chloe.

Tony Merida is the founding pastor of Imago Dei Church in Raleigh, N.C. He also serves as associate professor of preaching at Southeastern Baptist Theological Seminary. Tony holds a Ph.D. in preaching and a Master of Theology, both from New Orleans Baptist Theological Seminary. He is the author of *Faithful Preaching* (2009) and *Proclaiming Jesus* (2012), as well as the co-author of *Orphanology* (2011). He serves as a general editor and contributor for the Christ-Centered Exposition commentary series. He is married to Kimberly, with whom he has five adopted children.

Russell D. Moore is President of the Ethics & Religious Liberty Commission of the Southern Baptist Convention. He earned a B.S. in history and political science from the University of Southern Mississippi. He also received a Master of Divinity in biblical studies from New Orleans

Baptist Theological Seminary and a Ph.D. in systematic theology from The Southern Baptist Theological Seminary. He is the author of five books, including *Tempted and Tried: Temptation and the Triumph of Christ* (2011), *Adopted for Life: The Priority of Adoption for Christian Families and Churches* (2009), and *The Kingdom of Christ: The New Evangelical Perspective* (2004). He and his wife Maria are the parents of five boys.

Trillia Newbell is the consultant on Women's Initiatives for the Ethics & Religious Liberty Commission of the Southern Baptist Convention. She also serves as Lead Editor for Karis, the women's channel for the Council on Biblical Manhood and Womanhood. She is the author of *United: Captured by God's Vision for Diversity* (2014), and her writings have been featured by numerous publications and websites. She blogs at trillianewbell.com. Trillia lives near Nashville with her husband, Thern, and their two children.

David Prince has been Pastor of Preaching and Vision at Ashland Avenue Baptist Church in Lexington, Ky., since 2003. In addition to his role at Ashland, he is also an associate professor for Christian preaching and pastoral ministry at The Southern Baptist Theological Seminary in Louisville, Ky. He received his Master of Divinity from Southwestern Theological Seminary and his Ph.D. from The Southern

Baptist Theological Seminary. He is married to Judi and they have eight children: three boys and five girls.

Jimmy Scroggins is the lead pastor of Family Church in West Palm Beach, Fla., and previously served as dean of Boyce College and as teaching pastor at Highview Baptist Church. He holds a Ph.D. and Master of Divinity from The Southern Baptist Theological Seminary in Louisville, Ky. He is married to Kristin and they have eight children.

Kevin L. Smith serves as assistant professor of preaching at The Southern Baptist Theological Seminary and as teaching pastor at Highview Baptist Church in Louisville, Ky. Before moving to Highview, Kevin served as pastor for Watson Memorial Baptist Church for eight years. He is currently a Ph.D. candidate. In 2006, he became the first African-American ever elected Vice President of the Kentucky Baptist Convention. Kevin and his wife Patricia have been married for twenty-one years and have five children.

Andrew Walker is Director of Policy Studies at the Ethics & Religious Liberty Commission of the Southern Baptist Convention. Previously, he worked in the DeVos Center for Religion and Civil Society at the Heritage Foundation in Washington, D.C. He is a graduate of Southwest Baptist University and earned his Master of Divinity from The

Southern Baptist Theological Seminary. He is marred to Christian, and they have one daughter.

CONTENTS

≡ 1 ≡
WALKING THE LINE: THE GOSPEL AND MORAL PURITY

RUSSELL MOORE

Luke 3:2-22

Several weeks after assuming the presidency of the ERLC, I had a conversation that proved to be determinative for me in many ways. It was a conversation with a woman best described as spiritual, but not religious. She was someone who believed in spirituality, but she couldn't be confident that there was a God, and she was certainly not an evangelical. This woman wanted to talk to me about things we believe as Christians and as evangelicals. Most of her questions had to do with the Christian sexual ethic because these are the sort of things that are often discussed in our culture. Why do Christians believe this about sex? Why do Christians *not* believe this about sex?

When I answered all of her questions she said, "What you have to understand is that I don't know anyone who believes the things that you all believe about sexuality. Those things sound incredibly strange to me: that there would be people you would be attracted to or in a relationship with and you wouldn't have sex with them."

My response was to say, "I know that! And I believe in even stranger things than this. I believe a previously dead man is going to show up in the sky on a horse."

The central claim of Christianity does not sound normal when it is being proclaimed. As a matter of fact, the typical reaction when the gospel was being proclaimed in Galilee, Judea, and Jerusalem and then as the gospel marched forward in the book of Acts was for people to say: This sounds insane to us. It seems as though you have lost your mind because you believe these things—that this ex-corpse is now the ruler of the entire universe and that every knee shall bow and every tongue confess Jesus Christ is Lord to the glory of God the Father. That does not seem normal.

We are moving into a time in this country and in many places around the world where a Christian understanding of sexuality will seem strange and even subversive to the people around us. What I think we should do as the people of God is not run away from the strangeness of Christianity but to *reclaim* the strangeness of Christianity and focus on a crucified and resurrected Jesus Christ. The way that we will be able to speak to the people in our increasingly sexually-confused culture is not by more culture war posturing but by a Christ-shaped counterrevolution that takes seriously what the Bible speaks about sexuality, about marriage, and about human dignity and focuses that upon the gospel of Jesus Christ.

Luke 3:2-22 is a passage that focuses on an account of John the Baptist, a prophet who is speaking words to the people around him. When some people in our day and in our context describe themselves as "prophetic," it often means "like a jerk." They simply mean, "I'm speaking to you exactly what I have on my mind, but if I say it's prophetic, then it's spiritual and you can't really say anything to me about it." But that's not the way that the Bible defines "prophetic." Biblically defined, the *message* and the *mission* of a prophet is to speak words that have been given to provide a word of revelation and, as God says to the prophet Jeremiah, to tear down and to plant, to build up and to reconstruct. Furthermore, the Scriptures also tell us that though John the Baptist was the greatest of all the prophets until the coming of Christ, Jesus says that the least in the kingdom of God is greater than he. Ultimately, the mission of John the Baptist is the same mission given to us: to point and to say, "Behold the Lamb who takes away the sins of the world."

Now, what that means is we must understand what is happening in the world around us. We have to understand that we are part of a world in which something has gone terribly wrong. And we have to understand that as we speak prophetically within the church and outside of the church on issues of sexuality—or any other issue—we must do that in a way that opposes the devil without acting like the devil. It's easy to demonize opponents; it's difficult to oppose demons. Scripture says that we have been called to wrestle not against flesh and blood but against principalities and powers in the heavenly places. And one of the easiest things we can do is to decide that we will somehow fight like the devil in order to please the Lord. Remember, Jesus rebuked Peter—saying "Get behind me, Satan" when Peter, though attempting to do the work of Christ, was actually bypassing the cross and empowering the powers of darkness. And as we take the mission that we have been given and see the changes that are happening in the culture around us, it would be easy for us to do much the same thing. But the Scriptures call us to a different way. Jesus says that he, by the power of the cross, has bound the strongman and therefore he may plunder his house. You and I have to understand that the powers at work around us in this universe are working in two ways, and we must oppose both of those ways at the same time.

We live in a world in which untold numbers of people in our own congregations are enslaved to pornography. We live in a world where someone just blocks from you is contemplating walking away from a marriage or family. We live in a time where right now there is a young woman looking at two lines on a pregnancy test and wondering whether or not she should have that child eradicated from her life. We live in a world where children have unspeakable things done to them by predatory adults. We live in a world where many of our young women are being told implicitly and explicitly to see themselves to see their entire identity in terms of their sexual attractiveness and availability to men. We live in a world where concepts of marriage, love, fidelity, and family are contested at every turn. And it would be easy for the people of God to respond to all of that with handwringing. It would be easy for the people of God to respond with panic. It would be easy for the people of God to respond with surrender. And it would be easy for the people of God to respond with simple outrage. But we are the people who have been given a mission, which means we understand what is going on in the universe and that we are to wrestle principalities and powers through the cross.

The power of darkness is a power that comes first of all through deception. And that is exactly what John is addressing in Luke 3:2-22. John stands up and speaks a word that calls the people around him to repentance: You are walking in a way that seems right to you. Turn, and be reconciled to God! From the very beginning we see that the devil's power is, first of all, to deceive: Has God really said? Has God really spoken? Is the word of God really clear on these issues? And then secondly to declare that there is no accountability: You will not surely die. There will be no judgment for you.

I don't know of any man or any woman in any situation I've ever dealt with who first concluded that an extra-marital affair would be an excellent thing to do and then went out to find somebody with whom to have such an affair. Most of the time, there is a slow and gradual process in which a person is led and directed by his (or her) own heart and by circumstances to a place where that person now finds justification for why in this case, in this instance, in this circumstance it is acceptable and alright. The power of the evil one is to say that God has not clearly spoken and God will not clearly hold you accountable for this. You are able to be a god, discerning good and evil in your own life, while at the same time you are simply an animal driven along by instincts and not driven and directed by the word of God.

But John speaks honestly about the revelation of God and about the judgment that is coming. He speaks forcefully and urgently in a line that has to be one of the most astounding in all of Scripture. In verse 18, after John the Baptist has stood up and talked about unquenchable fire, Luke says this: "So with many other exhortations he preached good news to the people." *Good* news? He is telling them that they are under the judgment of God: "You brood of vipers! Who warned you to flee from the wrath to come?" I have never in my life stood up in a preaching assignment and said, "You bunch of snakes, who warned you to get out of the way of the judgment of God?" But John does, and Luke says this is good news. He is speaking good news to the people.

God has given a word. The word that calls to repentance is a word that does not leave us alone in the path we want to follow on our own. If Scripture is right that there is a judgment and if Scripture is right that the human conscience testifies to that coming judgment, then the refusal to speak to those consciences clearly and openly is a refusal to love. If the Apostle Paul is right when he says that sexual impurity is a sin against one's own body and that those who practice such things will not inherit the kingdom of God, the question is why? And Scripture tells us why: The sexual union isn't simply a biological act. It isn't simply the rubbing of body parts together to fire neurons and have a sensory experience. What Scripture tells us is that in the sexual union there is a joining together of a one-flesh union, which means something is happening spiritually. Paul says that your body is a temple of the Holy Spirit. When that body is being given over sexually, something is happening within the temple of God, and the temple is not simply an edifice. It isn't simply a building. It isn't simply a geographic point. The temple is the place where God is, marked out by its holiness. There are deep spiritual realties involved in the sexual act, which is why the Apostle Paul speaks so clearly to it. It's the reason why John, when he finds himself before Herod, speaks to the issue of Herod's sexual infidelity and sexual immorality. If you and I have been given the mission to speak to the world outside of us, calling them to Christ, and to speak to the world inside of the church, calling one another to holiness, then we must understand the stakes of the judgment seat of Christ. And we must speak every word that has been given to us.

It seems that every time any conversation comes up about issues of sexual morality, the question always turns into this: If only we would give up a Christian sexual ethic then we would be able to reach the next generation. Millennials would be able to receive the gospel. What's holding them back is that we are clinging to a sexual ethic that is antiquated and unrealistic, and this is the reason why they are not coming into our churches.

Now, on the one hand, it's untrue that we are losing a younger generation. But even if it were true, this is the exact same argument that has been used over and over and over again about parts of the Christian revelation that has been given to us. In the twentieth century the message was this: If only you could give up those bizarre miracle accounts, then you would be able to save Christianity and reach the scientifically enlightened people who want to follow Jesus. They want to believe in Jesus, but they just can't accept a virgin birth because they are too educated for that. The problem with this is, first of all, no one can accept a virgin birth easily. The people in the time of Jesus were not biologically ignorant. When Mary came to Joseph and said, "I'm pregnant," Joseph's response was not, "Well, it's beginning to look a lot like Christmas!" His response was, understandably, to accuse her of cheating on him.

The miraculous element of Christianity has always been seen as strange, but without the miraculous element of Christianity you have exactly what J. Gresham Machen saw in the liberalism of the 1920s: A different religion and a different gospel than the gospel of Jesus Christ. We do not have the power to adjust the biblical revelation the way we adjust the constitution and bylaws of our congregations. We are not making this up. We are delivering to a new generation what we have also received, which means that we speak honestly. We speak truthfully about what it means to follow Christ, including what it means to follow Christ sexually, even when that message is seen to be a difficult one to follow.

The Bible gives us several examples of people who are confronted by the word of God through John. And they are people who were fitting in very well within the culture around them: tax collectors and soldiers. And these people, the scripture says, are asking a very important question when they are confronted with the prophetic preaching of John: What then must we do? What does it mean to follow Christ? The gospel that is being given is not a gospel that is simply about mental ascent. It is about coming under the lordship of Christ, which means we must ask: How is this new lordship going to change the direction that I want to go?

The world around us is not built upon an imperial cult, but it is often built upon a Dionysian understanding of what it means to pursue one's sexual freedom and one's sexual autonomy. Ultimately, the question remains the same: As the message is preached, what then must we do? An "almost-gospel" is no match for the sexual revolution. And we have had, for too long and in too many of our circles, an almost-gospel.

In some Amish communities there is the concept of Rumspringa, which is the understanding that in that community children are raised up to live as Amish, but when they reach a certain age in late adolescence, they are able to leave the community and experience anything that they think they might miss later on. At the end, they decide whether they want to come back or whether they want to become part of the outside world. There was even an attempt several years ago to build a reality show around the idea of Rumspringa with Amish kids smoking cigarettes for the first time and getting drunk for the first time and having illicit sex for the first time. The problem is that we have a sort of Rumspringa in conservative evangelical circles too. For a long time, we have assumed that there will come a certain point in the lives of the people in our congregations when they will walk away from the faith that has been given to them. They will give themselves over to the pursuit of whatever sort of pleasure and success they wish to seek. And then after they get married, settle down, and start having children, they will come back into the church because they want to have a church with programs for their children. They are now normal citizens and normal church members and the process starts all over again.

The problem is that this is not the church that Jesus said he would build. The church that Jesus said he would build is a colony of the kingdom of God that is different from the ambient culture around it and points the ambient culture to a day in which the kingdoms of this world become the kingdom of our Lord and of his Christ. We have lived with the expectation that we can simply call for mental ascent to the facts of the gospel and then, when people are ready to settle back down into our routines, somehow we will be able to prevail against the gates of hell with a church like that. That is not the promise that Jesus has given.

We have also for too long, in many of our congregations and in many of our circles, held to a discount store prosperity gospel. I don't watch horror films. The closest I come is watching prosperity gospel preachers on TV. It gives me the same sort of adrenal rush. And one day on one program, there was a prosperity gospel teacher sitting on a golden throne (literally) with all sorts of rhinestones and purplish hair, and she said that even if the gospel of Jesus Christ were not true, she would still want to be a Christian because this is the best way to live. That is an easy thing to say from a golden throne on television. It's a difficult thing to say in Sudan. It's a difficult thing to say in China. It's a difficult thing to say in Ephesus, in Rome, in Jerusalem, in Judea. And when we are calling people to a Christian sexual ethic, if we have spent all of our time preaching a gospel that fulfills all the expectations that you already had of what it means to live your normal life your best life now with heaven at the end of it then of course it seems nonsensical to say to those that God has called to singleness that the path toward chastity is hard and difficult and rigorous. Of course it seems nonsensical to tell people who are tempted towards sexual immorality to fight and to struggle. Of course it seems nonsensical to say that a marriage ought not to be ripped apart when it becomes difficult and hard. And of course it seems nonsensical to say that the entire life of the Christian, whether that Christian is single or married, will be a life of spiritual warfare—including in those areas where the world, the flesh, and the devil conspire with biological impulses and urges to lead us toward our own destruction.

The gospel of Jesus Christ does not pretend that the path to sexual purity is easy. The gospel says that the entire life of the Christian is one of bearing our cross, which is why we need the entire body of Christ. Every single one of us is vulnerable at different points and vulnerable in different places and vulnerable in different ways, but all of us need the body of Christ so that the stronger bear up the weaker. All of us need a gospel—not an almost-gospel, but a whole gospel that speaks to us truthfully of God's justice and truthfully of God's justification to understand and to know the joy of what it means to follow and walk after Jesus.

When it comes to sexuality, we do not pretend as though this is something easily managed by willpower alone. God has designed the sexual drive to be powerful so that a man will leave his father and mother, cleave to his wife, and they shall become one flesh. There are all sorts of human civilizations that have died out for all sorts of reasons, but none has ever ceased to exist because people forgot to have sex. No one needs to send missionaries to teach people how to have sexual intercourse. God has placed a drive within human beings toward that one-flesh union because in that union he is showcasing, he is picturing, he is demonstrating the union of Christ and his church. The mystery that Paul is talking about in Ephesians 5 is then revealed. When you have a man who is giving himself to this woman, when you have a woman who is giving herself to this man and the two become one flesh, that is not just a relationship. It's a gospel tract. It is an invitation hymn. It is pointing us to something wild and mysterious: the relationship between Christ and the church.

So if we are going to be faithful Christians, if we are going to be people who are on mission, we cannot preach a different gospel than the gospel that Jesus has given to us. When those issues become difficult, Jesus and the apostles are constantly clarifying what the cost of discipleship is. When people in Galilee were responding to the gospel, Jesus was constantly turning around and saying: I don't think you understand what I just said. What I just said to a group of people who have been taught all their lives not to touch anything dead or to consume blood is that unless you chew my skin, unless you drink my blood, you can have no life in you. Jesus is clarifying that if you want to follow him you must understand the scandal and the strangeness of the gospel: I am not adjusting myself to your life plan. I am calling you into my life.

If we are to be faithful, we must oppose the deception that comes to every single one of us, including in the area of sexuality, and says that we can somehow work ourselves around the revelation that God has given us because there is something better than what God has given, something that we can grasp for ourselves. We must speak against that deception. If we don't do that, and we instead tell the culture what we think they want to hear or if we practice the sort of selective universalism that tells them what they want to hear only as it relates to sexuality we will not breed evangelism. We will breed cynicism from a group of people who will say, "If we cannot trust you to tell us the truth about your gospel, then how can we trust you to tell us how to be resurrected from the dead?"

We fight against deception, but the devil doesn't work only with deception. Scripture says that the devil has two powers: One of them is to deceive and the other is to accuse. No one is more pro-choice on the way into the abortion clinic than the devil, and no one is more pro-life on the way out of the abortion clinic than the devil. The powers of darkness want to deceive us and then stand and say, "We know who you are; we know what you have done." The mission that we have been given is a mission of good news. We do not preach a gospel of repentance alone; it is a message that frees people from the power of accusation through the blood of Jesus Christ. John is not simply saying, "You brood of vipers! Who warned you to flee from the wrath to come?" He stands and baptizes—including baptizing Jesus of Nazareth. When Jesus comes, John's first reaction is to say: No, I don't want to baptize you. Do you know why John doesn't want to baptize Jesus? Baptism is a mug shot of people who are guilty. You are agreeing with God that you are deserving of his condemnation. But Jesus asks to be baptized. Though without sin, he goes into the waters of baptism and identifies himself with sinners. John says that this is the one who takes away the sins of the world. The world doesn't need us to merely stand and speak about sexual immorality and sexual impurity. The devil is able to do that on his own. We have not been called simply to condemn; we have been called to reconcile. One of the pressing problems around us, including in the area of sexuality, is the power that the devil has over consciences in the area of accusation and blackmail of the heart.

We are living in a world full of sexual brokenness, where the devil is saying to people all around us, "I know who you are. I know what you've done." There are people in our communities who, like our first father and like our first mother, are hiding from the voice of God because of a word of accusation. But Christ came to seek and to save that which was lost, and he has given us that ministry of reconciliation. It is not enough to speak truthfully and to speak prophetically, including about issues of sexual morality. If we do not speak those words in continuity with our mission, then we are unfaithful to the mission that has been given to us. The Scriptures do not only warn us to flee immorality—they also say that the Lord's servant must not be quarrelsome. That doesn't mean that we don't fight. That doesn't mean that we don't struggle. It doesn't mean that we don't debate. It doesn't mean that we don't seek to persuade. But it means that we are not quarrelsome for the sake of arguments. We are seeking to speak as ambassadors of reconciliation to see people saved.

If the call to repentance does not end with the invitation that is grounded in the bloody cross and the empty tomb of Jesus, we are speaking a different word than the word that we have been given. And when we speak the gospel to those who are sexually broken in the world around us, we do so not only for their sake but also for ours. Jesus builds his church by redeeming sinners for himself. Jesus said, "Woman, where is your husband?" He doesn't leave her in the deception of thinking that she can move from husband to husband, from man to man with no accountability, but he also doesn't stand and speak a word of accusation and condemnation. He identifies the problem and then he invites her to living water. The church of the next generation must do that. We cannot simply call for repentance. We must say that those who practice such things will not inherit the kingdom of God, and we must say so clearly, and we must say so explicitly. We will find that if we speak with conviction and kindness, if we love the people around us, if we don't see them as super-villains, we will still make everyone mad. If you speak with conviction and call to repentance you will make people mad who don't want to repent. And if you speak with kindness and with love and if you live among those with whom you disagree, you will receive the anger of those who will say, "He eats with tax collectors and sinners." And you will be in very good company.

The call that we have is to love people enough to speak truthfully. How can you join Christ to an electronic prostitute? That means saying to the body of Christ: You are a chosen people, a royal priesthood. Your marriage is an icon of the union of Christ and his church. Your marriage is not your business alone.

It is the business of the entire people of God. We will love. We will admonish. We will minister. And when a marriage is being ripped apart we will discipline. And we will be the people who say to those on the outside: This is the message that has been given to us—God delights in the sexual union, but that sexual union is one that is found only in the lifelong union of one man to one woman in fidelity, in chastity, in love. And that is going to seem strange. That is going to seem freakish. And sometimes that is going to seem subversive. Our message ought to be: We understand; it seems strange to us too. But we believe even stranger things than that.

REVIEW QUESTIONS

1. *What are some of the devil's lies about sexuality that have taken hold in your community?*

2. *How can you and your church help instill a biblical view of sexuality in the hearts of fellow believers and their families?*

3. *What message would you give to believers who are struggling with feelings of condemnation and shame as a result of past sexual sin? How does the gospel of Christ speak directly to their situation?*

═ 2 ═
MARRIAGE MATTERS: CONTEMPORARY THREATS TO BIBLICAL MARRIAGE

ANDREW T. WALKER

G. K. Chesterton once wrote:

> The greatest political storm flutters only a fringe of humanity.
> But an ordinary man and an ordinary woman and their ordinary
> children literally alter the destiny of nations.

An ordinary man and an ordinary woman. Seems innocent enough.

But do you know the very first time God ever says something isn't good? It comes at the very beginning of his story and the significance of the statement likely wasn't lost on Chesterton:

> The Lord God said, "It is not good for the man to be alone. I will make a helper suitable for him." (Genesis 2:18)

> But for Adam no suitable helper was found. So the Lord God caused the man to fall into a deep sleep; and while he was sleeping, he took one of the man's ribs and then closed up the place with flesh. Then the Lord God made a woman from the rib he had taken out of the man, and he brought her to the man. (Genesis 2:20b–22)

The pairing of a man and a woman is the apex of God's craftsmanship. Man and woman are not accidental designs. Unlike the magnificent array of birds and trees and oceans, God created mankind "in his own image" (Genesis 1:27). And then God blessed them and told them to create a bunch of little Adams and Eves. This is the story of the world. From the foundation of every society, there stands a man and woman, uniting to bring forth new humanity. The author of Genesis makes a point of reminding us of the special relationship between one man and one woman. "That is why a man leaves his father and mother and is united to his wife, and they become one flesh" (Genesis 2:24).

When he was done, "God saw all that he had made, and it was very good" (Genesis 1:31). Not just good. *Very* good.

It is impossible to understand God's love for mankind or his plan for the world he created apart from marriage. God's plan for man and woman obviously impacts how we relate interpersonally, but it also determines how we order our communities. It changes our laws, the priorities we place on the uses of our time, and so much more.

Marriage is the unexamined assumption of our time, and most Christians enter marriage unaware of the effects when one man and one woman build a life together. It is an institution that people are expected to aspire to and to enter, but without the larger understanding of what their marriage can do to the community around them. Today, a typical Christian's understanding of marriage is unlikely to differ from everyone else's. The church has fed the great Myth of Marriage: a romance between best friends. With such vapid instruction from their religious leaders, it is no surprise that Christians are mired in divorce, infidelity, pornography, and other forms of sexual and relational brokenness.

But most Christians are unaware that marriage is changing as a social institution in America, evidenced by a decline in the marriage rate, a rise in cohabitation, couples waiting longer to marry, and the advent of same-sex unions. People's attitudes, their assumptions, and their expectations about the nature and institution of marriage are in flux. Consider the following realities:[1]

---

1   Peter Wehner, "Something That Was Not Imaginable 40 Years Ago Has Happened," *Commentary Magazine*, April 14, 2014. www.commentarymagazine.com

- In 1970, 83 percent of women aged thirty to thirty-four were married, but by 2010 that number had fallen to 57 percent. For almost every demographic group, whether broken down by age, education, race, or ethnicity, marriage rates have declined almost continuously since 1970.

- Marriage rates for twenty- to twenty-four-year-olds, for instance, fell from 61 percent to 16 percent, a decline of almost 75 percent in four decades.

- Non-marital births (that is, children born outside of wedlock) across all demographics have increased from 11 percent to nearly 41 percent of all households in America. In 2010 surveys revealed that upwards of 72 percent of all African American children were born into single-parent families.

- In 1970, only 12 percent of children lived in single-parent households, but over the next forty years that number increased by 124 percent, so that today 27 percent of all children live in such households.

- Incidentally, one of the greatest factors affecting poverty in America is whether a child is reared in a single-parent household. If we want to fix poverty and achieve justice in America, we need to talk about restoring the sanctity of marriage, not just from a Christian standpoint but from a social standpoint as well.

These are important variables for the church for one reason: What exists outside the church usually makes its way inside the church. Our response can be either to combat them or conform to them. In examining contemporary threats to marriage I will first consider snapshots, trends, and statistics to capture an overview of the national climate.

First, though, we need to define what biblical marriage actually is. Biblical marriage is the lifelong union of a man and a woman as husband and wife. It is oriented towards the creation of children. And in this definition we see the structure of marriage. It is complementary based on the sexes—a man and a woman. It's permanent, meaning that marriage begins with the assumption that it is to last the duration of a man and woman's collective lives. And it's exclusive or monogamous, confined to one adult man and one adult woman.

The biblical definition of marriage applies to all persons, regardless of their adherence to Christian principles. When non-Christians cooperate in marriage, they are experiencing a creational institution designed by God to prosper all persons. Some non-Christians would prefer to get the church out of marriage altogether; but as Christians, our arguments in favor of marriage extend beyond just the theological. Grounded in Scripture, the Christian understanding of marriage, understood through natural law principles, reveals its relevance for every society—whether it's heavily populated with Christians or not.

Biblical morality is human morality, and in turn, biblical marriage is human marriage. So if we establish the idea of "Christian marriage," we open the door for secularists or others to simply say, "That's exactly right. You just need to have Christian marriage and let the government have its separate concept of marriage." The problem, however, is that this is not how marriage is designed to function. If we set up marriage only as a theological institution, when it is much more, we could easily overlook the Bible's public purpose of marriage. And the Bible's purpose for marriage is intrinsically public by nature. The church's theology of marriage, while certainly ecclesial, isn't sectarian. Marriage leads one outside the laws of the church and into the public square because marriage, by design, reveals a certain purpose about us as having been made male and female. When we talk about marriage, we are actually talking about how God made humanity to function. I want to say it this way—marriage may be *ultimately* Christian, but it's not *exclusively* Christian, at least according to this era of redemptive history. At the same time, we can confidently assert that while non-Christians have the right to marry, marriage has its fullest meaning, expression, and fulfillment in the context of Christian marriage.

EXTERNAL THREATS TO MARRIAGE IN CULTURE

The first threat to marriage is what I am calling a soul mate or "happily ever after" conception of marriage. This view sees marriage as primarily an emotional fulfillment. It's based on a paradigm of marriage that sees its central importance as one of sexual enhancement and partnership.

I want to give you a little brief biography here to explain how we've all imbibed this paradigm of marriage. I attended a Southern Baptist college and a Southern Baptist seminary, both conservative institutions. I never learned or inherited an understanding of marriage that didn't center almost exclusively on marriage's connection to discipleship, romance, and personal holiness, all of which is correct. But then I went to work at a secular think tank, where my theology of marriage was confronted with the reality of marriage, its decline, and associated social ills. I grew up with this "happily ever after" idea of marriage but later learned that much of society's breakdown is related entirely to the breakdown of marriage. I sense that this is fairly common within evangelical communities. In all of our drive and enthusiasm to change the world, we overlook the role that marriage can play in fostering healthy, more vibrant communities.

Across the board, from educational outcome to financial outcome to emotional outcome, marriage plays a key factor in how children's lives affect their development into adulthood. Children do better on any range of measureable outcomes when raised in a home with a mom and a dad. Intact marriages create more emotionally balanced children who are less likely to experience divorce themselves. Children reared in households with a mother and father are dramatically less likely to experience poverty and incarceration and are more likely to graduate high school.

All things being equal, a child raised in a household with a mother and father, biological or not, stands a much better chance of succeeding, thriving, and flourishing into adulthood. When looking at the amount of government-assisted payouts throughout all seventy-nine means-tested federal and state welfare programs (an estimated $927 billion in 2011), it is hardly debatable that divorce and out-of-wedlock childbearing are two major factors contributing to America's vastly inflated welfare state.

Only after I worked at a secular institution was I able to connect the social purpose of marriage to its biblical foundation. Marriage is about romance and happiness, but it's also about channeling sexual desire in biblical ways oriented towards procreation. Ultimately, marriage is incredibly important to societal or social health. As pastors, we need to teach a view of marriage in our churches that includes its societal importance. In marriage counseling, we need to begin equipping couples with a broader, social understanding of marriage that incorporates the importance of marriage with the health of children and society.

If we base our view of marriage on the idea of personal happiness, togetherness, and sexual fulfillment, for example, we look insensitive and arbitrary when we exclude homosexuals from those benefits. It is only when marriage is connected with something larger than adult desire that we gain a roadmap to connecting marriage to society's health. If we want to make same-sex marriage unthinkable in society, heterosexuals need to do a better job of attaching marriage to its social basis. Moreover, the fleeting emotions that a "happily ever after" paradigm can easily foster won't be an adequate safeguard against marital discord. When a couple "falls out of love," as is common today, you can be sure that an overly idealized understanding of marriage pervaded their views on marriage.

Marriage exists to bring a man and woman together as husband and wife, to be father and mother to any children their union produces. Marriage attaches men and women to children. When a child is born, we *know* that a mother will be nearby. The question is whether the father will be. Marriage helps resolve that tension, binding mother and father to children.

To overcome these gaps in our thinking, we need to recapture the essence and purpose of marriage. Marriage is based on the truth that men and women are different and complementary, the biological fact that reproduction depends on a man and a woman, and the reality that children need a father and a mother. Marriage predates government. It's the fundamental building block of all human civilization. Marriage has public purposes that transcend private purposes, but of late marriage has been weakened by a revisionist view that is more about adults' desires than children's needs. This reduces marriage to a system that approves emotional bonds or distributes legal privileges among consenting adults.

Why does marriage matter for public policy? A growing number of Christians would prefer to bypass this contentious debate and allow the government to sanction civil marriage. Government recognizes marriage because it is an institution that benefits society in a way that no other relationship does. Marriage is society's best way to ensure the wellbeing of children, with minimal state involvement. If we want a smaller state and smaller taxes, we can encourage that by having and fostering a healthy marriage culture. While respecting everyone's liberty, government rightly recognizes, protects, and promotes marriage as the ideal institution for child-bearing and childrearing. Promoting marriage doesn't ban any type of relationship. Adults are free to make choices about their relationships and do not need government sanction to do so.

Secondly, biblical marriage is not only threatened by the "soul mate" concept of marriage, but the idea of marriage as an aspiration is also eroding the biblical construct. Marriage as an aspiration is a factor causing people to delay marriage. Today, we are told to think of marriage as the capstone to an already built career, to believe we will marry once we are financially established and our careers are in motion. But this encourages us to treat marriage like the capstone of adulthood, rather than evidence of having emerged into adulthood. This encourages us to delay marriage. This is not to promote marriage among seventeen-year-olds, nor to encourage sixteen-year-olds to drop out of school and get married. Rather, we push back against the expectation that someone needs two degrees and $50,000 or $100,000 in the bank in order to marry.

Third, economic pressures represent an enormous threat to marriage. Economic pressures prevent people from marrying and maintaining stability in marriage. College loan debt, for example, delays marriage and childbearing. Educational expenses drain funds that could otherwise cover the down payment on a house. Prolonged education in general is another economic pressure threatening biblical marriage. Education is good, of course, but there is this idea that education must be entirely complete before marriage can even be a possibility. I am living proof that you can have a spouse who has graduated while you yourself are still in college and still achieve a happy marriage. You may not have a lot of money, but you can have a great life married to the person you love. When I hear similar stories told by couples that married young, all reflect with nostalgia upon the humbleness of their beginnings, but somehow they were the happiest they'd have ever been, despite the economic circumstances. So you don't need to be twenty-nine and have thousands of dollars to marry, but neither would I suggest marriage at sixteen with only a paper route for income.

Biblical marriage is threatened by employment concerns related to economic pressures. If men lack stable employment with a decent income, statistics indicate that couples are much more likely to get divorced. Being underemployed is an impediment to marriage for males. Women find vocational and economic stability a key trait in marriage partners.

A fourth threat to biblical marriage is the rise of what I'm calling professional marriages. Here, couples lead parallel lives in which "one flesh" means merely sexual union, not a lifestyle union. Bank accounts and social lives are kept separate. Each person has entirely separate friends; they do separate things on the weekends. This may sound strange, but I know marriages that are like this. They are marriages in a legal sense, but as a way of lifestyle commitment, such marriages reduce to coexistence beneath one roof.

If you are married, you are to hold all things in common. One simple, practical step to help marriages foster a sense of holding all things in common is to share bank accounts. There shouldn't be separate bank accounts if you are married. You shouldn't be hiding money and assets from each other. Spending should be done out in the open. Professional marriages also put off children for the sake of amassing sums of money in order to be prepared. My wife and I had some friends in college that were older than us, probably in their mid-twenties, while we were in our early twenties. The husband in the relationship refused to have children until they had saved $100,000. Aside from the mistaken belief that average Americans have $100,000 lying around, it was truly sad because whenever he would bring this up, you could tell that his wife was just miserable. She was trying to honor her husband's financial planning; but let's just be honest—unhealthy financial expectations associated with marriage and childbearing crippled this marriage's happiness.

A fifth threat to biblical marriage is sexual liberation in general. Since the sexual revolution of the 1960s, sexual liberation has negated the concept that sex should be reserved for marriage. Our social context no longer has a taboo about sexual promiscuity; rather, such behavior is glorified. We live in an era of radically autonomous and individualized understandings of the human person. It's the "if it feels good do it" mentality. The principle of how this harms marriage in particular is that sexual freedom reduces the need to experience sex solely within the context of marriage itself. Another way of emphasizing this point is that the "goods" of marriage can now be experienced apart from marriage. Society, thanks to Hollywood exemplars, has largely turned a blind eye to out-of-wedlock childbearing. Whereas commitment and the sharing of one's life could formerly only take place within marriage, cohabitation has now made these features available without the need for marriage. Lastly, the taboo of promiscuity has largely abated, such that entering marriage as a virgin is now the exception rather the norm.

One story illustrates how rampant this view has become. I was back in my hometown a couple of years ago for my cousin's wedding, gathered with friends who attended my high school. It was a big high school reunion of sorts. At the wedding reception, I soon realized that I was the only one there in my age group who was married with children and who drove a minivan—not something that barhopping twenty-somethings typically do. These are badges of honor as much as they are evidence of having grown out of adolescence. A friend approached me and said, "Andrew, man, it seems like you have really made it in life, you know. You are married. You've got a kid. You know, you've got a job. And you've got a minivan." And I was like, "What? Thanks, I think." I would have assumed most of them would have been in the same boat as I, simply by default. But we have delayed marriage, or substituted the notion of cohabiting instead. When I learned that I was the only one at the wedding who had not lived with his wife prior to being married, I was floored. Cohabitation, it seems, is the norm.

Sixth, biblical marriage is threatened by same-sex marriage. How?

- If we redefine marriage as society is doing, the change will further distance marriage from the needs of children.

- Such a revision denies, as a matter of policy, the ideal that a child needs a mom and a dad. Social science supports that children tend to do best when raised in a household with a mother and a father.

- The confusion resulting from further disassociating childbearing from marriage would force the state to intervene more often in family life and cause welfare programs to grow even more.

- When discussing same-sex marriage, many are accustomed to trotting out the polygamy argument, which in principle is true.

But I don't find this an especially effective argument. Rather, I predict that the outcome of same-sex marriage's continued presence will be the further erosion or deinstitutionalization of marriage, such that marriage will become even less persuasive. Marriage is becoming less recognizable, because the norms of marriage, namely permanency, exclusivity, and complementarity are no longer intact.

The endgame of same-sex marriage is that fewer and fewer people will marry. Redefining marriage puts into the law a new principle that marriage is whatever emotional bond the government says it is. If marriage is no longer based on the complementarity of the sexes, why limit it to two persons? Why assume marriage must be permanent and exclusive? Already, individuals are proposing the establishment of "wed-leases." A column in The Washington Post advocated for term-limited marriages that are good for five to ten years.[2] At ten years they can be either renewed or shut down. The marriage would then dissolve if no action was taken. These types of proposals can only be advanced when a new marriage regime takes effect.

Same-sex marriage makes marriage less identifiable and more obscure. Law teaches belief. Belief shapes behavior. Over time, the normative structure of marriage will become

---

2 Paul Rampell, "A high divorce rate means it's time to try 'wedleases,'" *Washington Post*, August 4, 2013.

less necessary, less persuasive, and less identifiable. Redefining marriage does not simply expand the existing understanding of marriage. It rejects the truth that marriage is based on the biological fact that reproduction depends on a man and a woman and the reality that children need a mother and a father.

Redefining marriage is a direct and demonstrated threat to religious freedom in that it marginalizes those who affirm marriage as the union of a man and a woman. Today's greatest cultural debates center on First Amendment protections for religious freedom, buffeted by an individual's right to enter a same-sex marriage.

A seventh threat to biblical marriage is no-fault divorce. To be very clear, homosexuals did not ruin marriage; heterosexuals ruined marriage starting in the 1970s. The redefinition of marriage began long before same-sex marriage appeared on the political landscape. Whereas divorce was once permitted along the lines of the three "A's"—adultery, abuse, abandonment—no-fault divorce introduced a radical redefinition of marriage that discredited commitment. Begun in the 1970s, no-fault divorce, oddly enough, was billed as a way to make walking away from bad marriages easier. The problem is that it taught a new truth about marriage and the law—that marriage is really just a contract rather than a lifetime binding covenant. Typically, the law shapes belief about marriage and, in turn, shapes our behavior within marriage. We have an unending circular dialectic between law, culture, and policy; they all interact with one another.

INTERNAL THREATS TO MARRIAGE WITHIN THE CHURCH

Topping the list of internal threats to marriage is an inability at the local church level to preach about divorce. I originally wanted to say there's an indifference at the local level concerning messages on divorce. But I realize that's not the case. Divorce has become so common that churches find it difficult to discuss. This is not to indict anyone's ministry, but I think I can recall one sermon in the past decade that focused heavily on divorce. Not that we should preach about divorce fifty Sundays a year, but in the context of marriage, when we talk about Ephesians 5, for example, or Genesis 2, we need to use these opportunities to preach about the significance of divorce in general. We need to do so with grace and truth. We need to reawaken ourselves to the fact that divorce obscures the gospel. We need to recognize that if God had a no-fault divorce mechanism available, there would be no gospel. The gospel is permanent, constant, and exclusive, and we see those patterns borne out in marriage in Genesis 2 and Ephesians 5.

A second internal threat to marriage is the local church's inability to connect marital fidelity to church membership. In some contexts, church membership requires as much information and commitment as a membership at Sam's Club. You sign on the dotted line. You commit to entering through its doors on a regular basis, and you are in good standing. I think that's problematic.

I think membership ought to have a higher threshold for entry. Pastors ought to be asking potential members questions about their past and about how past actions impact their present. Were they divorced? If so, on what grounds were they divorced? If it is discovered that the person inquiring about church membership has had an affair and remains unrepentant, that ought to be an impediment to that person being received into a local church. One way to enhance our internal and external witness on marriage is to intensify our accountability structure. This is not to make the barrier to church membership impenetrable, but simply to connect our desire for strengthening marriage to our church governance.

Third, biblical marriage further threatened by the lack of a culture of marriage mentoring within the church. I have been very encouraged to see the depth at which some pastors are conducting and requiring pastoral counseling. I would say: Great! Let's double it or triple it or quadruple it. We will have prospective candidates for marriage who will spend hundreds of hours preparing for a wedding but maybe four hours preparing for the actual marriage through marriage counseling. We need to redouble our efforts to mentor those who want a pastor to perform the wedding. There ought to be programs to connect older, faithful couples as mentors to younger couples during the first year or six months of the younger couples' marriages.

Fourth, the church's failure to connect the authority of the gospel to the uniqueness of marriage threatens the biblical definition of marriage. In all we do, we must stress that marriage is the one institution that God gave to the world which somehow pictures the gospel. As the gospel demonstrates the unconditional love of God in Christ, so does marriage. As God demonstrates his love toward us, so we must love our spouse. As God absorbs all wrongdoing, as he reconciles and forgives, so must we behave towards our spouse. As God looks upon his church with purity and holiness, so must we look upon our spouse. Satan hates marriage because it's a tangible picture of the gospel. If you look at Genesis 2 and Ephesians 5, it's clear that God promised salvation through a vehicle of marriage. In Ephesians 5, Paul is adamant that marriage incarnates the mystery of the gospel. Therefore we shouldn't be surprised that Satan would attack a marriage culture.

AUTHORITY, NARRATIVE, WITNESS

I want to suggest a template we might employ to recover a healthy biblical culture in our churches. This template involves authority, narrative, and witness. We must recover the authority of the gospel over marriage. We need to embed it in the narrative and live it out by a congregational witness. We must always engage marriage on the plane of the absolute highest authority. God in his gospel determines marriage; it is not for the government to define. "Traditional marriage" is no longer an acceptable phrase. Tradition is not a moral category. In fifty or a hundred years, same-sex marriage will be considered traditional. A more preferable term might be natural marriage, but even that phrase isn't particularly well grounded in authority. Marriage must always be grounded in the Christ-church narrative. Marriage can no longer just be a Genesis 2 issue. Marriage is also a Romans 1 issue and an Ephesians 5 issue, in which society's abandonment and rejection of God's sexual standard is linked with humanity's self-willed social misery. Discussions of marriage must always be paired with the gospel. We must be clear about the gospel's demand for our sexual ethics, but we must not forget to equally preach that what the gospel demands, the gospel empowers to accomplish.

In addition to the authority of the gospel over marriage, we have to establish a narrative on marriage; that is, we must understand marriage's gospel purpose and its social scope. That is the narrative. Any movement must have storytellers who tell the story accurately, with gravitas and imagination. Only the gospel grounds the narrative in any story we want to tell about marriage. Authority and narrative must be lived out in the flesh. This is our witness. We must boldly proclaim that God's sexual design is for our good. We must understand that correcting marriage in society begins with churches committing to correct marriage internally, within the walls of the church. This requires both the church universal and the local church. We must frame marriage in the context of a postmodern sexuality that will likely respond to our sexual ethics with humiliation and mockery. So be it. As Peter Leithart has said regarding the Christian sexual ethic and its estrangement from mainstream culture, "We are approaching the fragrance of martyrdom on marriage and Christian sexuality."

THE CALL TO BE AN ORDINARY RADICAL

So we must live out the public purpose of marriage as a local community that experiences the flourishing of the Bible promises associated with marriage. But how do we do this? We do it by virtue of courage, because it is Spirit-infused courage alone that allows us to put authority, narrative, and witness into action.

The vision for marriage we want to see lived out isn't radical. It's extravagantly ordinary. It's found in that moment where a child or spouse is sick, disrupting our plans, and the choice must be made to serve others rather than self. Furthermore, we're calling on pastors, youth pastors, and college administrators—anyone in a place of authority with the ability to restore and communicate the significance of marriage to our communities—to step out and do it. Keep marriage on the front of the public mind. Embrace the power of the local. Kill cynicism. Crucify apathy. Refuse to allow your friends, children, and church to accommodate to our flaccid marriage culture. For the sake of the gospel's integrity and consistency, have the courage to confront the errors of our day, not because we're outraged moralists, but because the future of individuals and the society they are maturing into is at stake.

REVIEW QUESTIONS

1. *How is the "happily ever after" conception of marriage seen in our culture? What problems can that create?*

2. *What benefits does honoring God's design for marriage bring to a society?*

3. *How should Christians in today's rapidly changing culture respond to the challenge of same-sex marriage?*

4. *How can our churches overcome the problem of widespread divorce among our members? How can we help couples strengthen their marriages?*

═ 3 ═
MENDING FENCES:
THE GOSPEL AND PASTORAL
CARE FOR SEXUAL SIN

J.D. GREEAR

Some of the biggest issues we have to deal with involve what the Bible teaches about sex and what the Bible has to say to people who make sexual mistakes. There are few things that make the Christian message more offensive and out of sync with culture. I saw a survey recently that showed sexual ethics to be the number one reason that students lose their faith in college. The second is what they call the problem of evil—why would a good God allow this or that to happen. But the number one reason why people depart from the faith in college is the desire for sexual freedom. I feel like this is something that we as a church have to deal with constantly. But I also know that there are few things that get at the heart and the gospel like sexuality because our sexuality goes down to the core of our beings.

Years ago Josh McDowell made this statement: He said that our culture thinks that sex is the answer, but, if anything, it is probably better understood as the question. Our society wants to present sexuality as pure biology. It's like food. When you are hungry, you eat. Or it's a sport. Where and how do you like to play? And so the only relevant sexual questions that we need to ask are, you know, what works for you? What kind of food do you prefer? What kind of sports do you like? But here are some questions that we have to ask our society to consider: If sex is just biology, if it's just recreational fun, then why is it that when a child is sexually abused, and then when he becomes an adult and is finally able to connect the dots of how all this happened, why is it so difficult to shake off? It's not just that an authority figure betrayed him. It's deeper than that. Why is rape so much more harmful to a woman than simply being beat up? Women will report physical abuse, but they will rarely, or at least much less often, report rape. Why is adultery so hard to overcome in a relationship? Why is it that men with the deepest sexual issues usually had uninvolved or missing fathers? Why is it that people's greatest regrets are so often of a sexual nature? Sex is not just physical. It's more. It goes to the core of who we are.

I want to share four principles for pastors and Christian teachers. That's what I am. I'm not a licensed counselor. I'm a pastor.

1. MAINTAIN THE HIGH GROUND IN DISCUSSIONS ABOUT SEXUALITY.

People in our society think that the Christian view of sex is low and that their own is very high. They recognize sex to be about freedom, enjoyment, and self-expression. And people of faith are trying to restrict all that for no good reason. The people of Paul's day thought the exact same thing. When Paul talked about sex he quoted a common proverb of the day: "Food is meant for the stomach and the stomach for food" (I Cor. 6:13). In other words, it's just biology. That's what it's made for. Food is made for the stomach. The stomach is made for food. The implication is that sex is made for the genitals, and the genitals are made for sex. It's really nothing more than that. That's the proverb that evidently was common among the Corinthians. That's what Paul addresses. He then spends several verses telling you why it's not true. Verse 16: "Or do you not know that he who is joined to a prostitute becomes one body with her? For, as it is written, 'The two will become one flesh.'" In other words, he is taking a higher view of sex than the Corinthians. It's not just biology, he says. There's a "one-flesh-ness" that happens in sex—the two become one.

He continues in verse 18, "Flee from sexual immorality. Every other sin a person commits is outside the body, but the sexually immoral person sins against his own body." Most sins that we commit, Paul says, are outside the body. If I steal from you, then I am actually harming you. That's what makes it sin, right? But sex outside of marriage is also a sin against ourselves, against our own bodies.

God designed us to be psychosomatic beings, body-soul beings, in which the physical oneness of sex is to be accompanied by oneness in every other area: financial oneness, spiritual oneness, and emotional oneness for life. The union of bodies apart from union in all the other areas is not fully human. It's only part. You've separated body and soul. You have separated things that God never intended to be separate. It's half human. Like a zombie. That's what makes a zombie scary: it looks like a human, but it doesn't have a soul. That is what is grotesque about sex outside of the marriage union. The problem, Paul says to a pagan world, is not that *I* don't recognize the beauty and power of sex. The problem is that *you* don't really recognize the power and beauty of sex.

I often tell students that when somebody wants to have sex with them outside of marriage, they are essentially saying, "I want your body right now, but I don't really want you." Even if they say, "I love you," if they have made no commitment to you then they could walk away at any moment because they just don't desire to be in that kind of permanent union yet. C. S. Lewis had a great analogy for this: He said the guy who wants to have sex with a girl without marrying her is like the guy who likes to taste food, but then regurgitate it. I want the meal, but I don't want the saturated fats and empty calories that go along with it, so I am going to taste the meal, then throw it up so I don't carry it with me. Paul says that sex outside the context of a full and complete union is not just a sin against God, and it's not just a sin against another person; it's a sin against you because it tears apart the integrity of the person. It disintegrates you.

A few years ago I read a book called *Hooked*. It is a scientific study written by a couple of neurologists that shows what having multiple sexual partners when you are young does to your brain. It actually rewires your brain in a way that makes genuine, lasting, selfless relationships much more difficult in the future. As far as I know, they did not write it as a Christian book. They just wrote it as a scientific study from a neurological perspective. They might be Christians, I'm not sure, but it's not written with that agenda. Here's what they say in there: The individual who goes from sex partner to sex partner is causing his or her brain to mold in such a way that it eventually accepts that sexual pattern as normal. The pattern of changing sex partners therefore seems to damage their ability to bond in a committed relationship. The kind of attachment damage that occurs after repeated sexual encounters is in many respects, they say, more pernicious than pregnancy or STDs because it typically goes unperceived by affected individuals while causing ongoing difficulties in establishing a lifelong and satisfying relationship.

If you take a strip of duct tape and wrap it around somebody's arm, it will adhere to the hair on their arm. If you then rip off that piece of duct tape, you are going to have pieces of their arm and hair come with it. But if you take that same piece of duct tape and do it to someone else, you will still take off pieces of hair and skin, but it's going to be less, until eventually the tape has lost all of its stickiness and it no longer has the ability to adhere. That is the analogy the authors of *Hooked* use to explain how the brain actually rewires, making real lifelong commitment impossible. Here's what the authors say:

> You can no more try out sex than you can try out birth. The very act of sex produces a new reality that cannot be undone.[1]

In other words, we have students at our church, young professionals, people of all ages—but especially students—who don't want to wait to have sex until they are married because they are afraid that they will miss out on something. What Paul is trying to say is that God is telling you not to have sex precisely because he *doesn't* want you to miss out on something, and that something is the ability to be in this kind of covenant relationship.

I want to be very careful not to approach these subjects in a way that suggests that people should only obey God because his way makes pragmatic sense, because if that is the criteria of obedience, we are never going to get anywhere. We obey God because he is the Creator and he makes the rules. But our Creator has reasons for his rules. He created the world the way he did so that it would operate in *shalom*. It is the most human form of living. You are most alive when you are living according to his pattern. Sex is a beautiful

---

1   Joe S. McIlhaney, *Hooked: New Science on How Casual Sex is Affecting Our Children* (Chicago: Northfield Publishing, 2008).

thing, created by God to add to human flourishing. And he gives us a taste of his beauty, his nature, his bliss, and his love. God created sex to lead us to worship, to glorify our Creator in the very best things that we get to experience on earth. Taking it outside of that context produces an equal amount of devastation.

We should never surrender that high ground in discussions on sexuality. In fact, we need to aggressively pursue that high ground. Sex is one of God's most powerful earthly gifts—it is a renewal of the covenant. When a man and his wife have sex together, they are renewing the covenant that they made when they said, "I do." God designed it to be a statement of that covenant, and to remove it from the context of that covenant makes it less than human. Tim Keller says while sex outside of marriage may lead to shouts of ecstasy, inside of marriage it leads to tears of joy, which makes the shouts of ecstasy look like cheap thrills.

2. EXPOSE THE ROOT SINS BEHIND SEXUAL SIN.

Paul says in Romans 1 that the sin behind all other sins is idolatry. A layman's definition of idolatry is this: Idolatry is when you love something, trust something, or obey something more than God. All sins, Paul says in Romans 1:23, end up going back to idolatry, and that seems to be especially true with sex.

In the gospel of John, Jesus dealt with two women in sexual sin. The first one is in John 4. Jesus encounters a woman in Samaria. He strikes up a conversation with her and asks her if she would give him water. She says: Why are you talking to me? You're a Jew!

Jesus answers her, "If you knew the gift of God, and who it is that is saying to you, 'Give me a drink,' you would have asked him, and he would have given you living water." He then goes on to explain in verse 13, "Everyone who drinks of this water will be thirsty again, but whoever drinks of the water that I will give him will never be thirsty again. The water that I will give him will become in him a spring of water welling up to eternal life."

Now, you and I know that he wasn't talking about actual water, but she didn't know that. Jesus asks her to go get her husband so they could all talk about what this living water looks like. She stares at the ground and says she doesn't have a husband. Her soul is thirsty and so she has gone to the well of romantic love, not one time or two times, but five times. She has given up on the institution of marriage and is just romantically involved with a guy. Her soul is in the same condition as her body. But Jesus tells her that he's not talking about physical water. The reason she has been driven to adultery and serial monogamy is because her soul is thirsty. Sexual cravings spring from a deep soul dissatisfaction.

What does a drowning man do to a five-foot-two, brown-headed life preserver? He clings to it, and suffocates the life out of it, because he is desperate to keep himself out of the sea of all those things. That's why they become codependent. That's why it doesn't work, because problems like loneliness and insecurity and low self-esteem were not designed to be cured by another human being. They were designed to be cured only by the love of God.

The first effect of our sin in the Garden of Eden was a sense of our nakedness. We actually were naked before we sinned, but the early church fathers said that our nakedness did not bother us because we were clothed in the love and the acceptance of God. But having sinned, we were stripped from that love. What do naked people do? They seek covering. What do thirsty people do? They seek water. Sex became a kind of covering. There is a deep craving in us for unity, for redemption, for satisfaction, for bliss and ecstasy, and sex seems like a good means toward that.

One of the clearest testimonies to this comes from the pen of a Jewish agnostic named Ernest Becker in his book *The Denial of Death*. He said that after he quit believing in God he still found his soul searching for acceptance and validation:

> Modern society, after having ceased to believe in God, turned to the romantic partner as the replacement. The self-glorification that we need in our innermost being, we now look for in the love partner. The love partner becomes the divine ideal with which to fulfill one's life. What is it that we want when we elevate the love partner to this position? We want to be rid of our faults. We want to be rid of our feeling of nothingness. We want to be justified. We want to know that our existence has not been in vain. We want redemption, nothing less. In case we are inclined to forget

how deified the romantic love object is, the popular songs continually remind us.[2]

When attacking any sin, you must expose the root, which is idolatry. G. K. Chesterton said, "Every man who knocks on the door of a brothel is looking for God." He realized that there is something much deeper going on there. Now, a lot of people don't see how that connects to idolatry. It doesn't seem like an idol. The problem is not that our sexual desires are too strong. The problem is that our love for God is so weak that we would have more regard for her father than we would for the Almighty God of the universe. It is because God is so small that our sexual passions are so captivating. That's idolatry. Idolatry is when something commands my obedience more than God because it consumes my imagination more than God.

In *The Sickness Unto Death*, Søren Kierkegaard says that idolatry is whenever you build your identity on anything but God or whenever you derive ultimate fulfillment from anything other than God. That's idolatry. When you tell a world that has abandoned religion that they should not do something because "thus says the Lord," they will immediately put up a wall and resist. But when you can demonstrate that they are building their identity on something, when you can show them that they are seeking fulfillment in something, that will actually get at their hearts a whole

2   Ernest Becker, *The Denial of Death* (New York: Free Press, 1997).

lot quicker than simply giving them a list of do's and don'ts. Kierkegaard is not saying, and I am certainly not saying, that we should not preach the commandments or preach the authority of the Bible. I am simply saying that we ought to help unpack the human heart and show people: You are expressing some deep desires. You're worshiping at the altar of romantic love, just like this woman in John 4, and it's not working for you. That's why you are moving from partner to partner, and that is why you are unhappy with the partner you are with today.

3. SHOW THE MULTIFACETED BEAUTY OF THE GOSPEL TO DEAL WITH SEXUAL SIN.

Jesus showed the woman in John 4 that living water would come from knowing his everlasting love. A lot of Jewish scholars point out that in those days the well was where people would go on dates. That was where marriages were arranged. The fact that Jesus met this woman at a well was indicating something to her. He was showing her that he was the true bridegroom, that she could worship in spirit and in truth—which is a very important phrase because her love had not been spirit. Because her soul has been so damaged she no longer knew how to really unite with a guy. Jesus shows her what she is looking for, that she could know God's love in spirit and in truth.

At the core of the human desire is a longing to be known and loved. To be known but not loved is rejection. To be loved but not really known is just sentimentality. But to be known and loved is the fulfillment of our deepest human desires. However, it presents a dilemma for us. We think, "If you really knew all there is to know about me, surely you wouldn't love me." That's the condition the woman is in. "If you knew what I know, then you wouldn't want to be close to me." The gospel that Jesus is preaching to this woman is that he knows you fully. He knows you better than you know yourself. He bore your sin so that he could know you fully and love you entirely, and he could not love you any more extravagantly than that.

Perhaps the clearest demonstration of this is what Jesus said in John 8. A woman is caught in the act of adultery, and so she is brought by the Jewish leaders into the city square, where they are going to stone her. But they are also trying to trap Jesus. They ask him what they should do with the woman. Jesus says to them, "Let him who is without sin among you cast the first stone." They all look at each other awkwardly, drop the rocks, and go home. Then Jesus looks at the woman and says to her, "Neither do I condemn you. Go and sin no more."

Here is what is odd to me about Jesus' statement: I would almost always reverse those two clauses. I would say, "If you go and sin no more, then I won't condemn you." But Jesus was showing the woman that his acceptance comes first. She was not to change *in order* to be accepted; she was changed because she *had been* accepted. Acceptance first, change second. He knew she could never break free of the idolatry that led her to adultery until she had felt the embrace of a God that was better than romance, a love more fulfilling than sex. She was likely in the same condition as the woman in John 4. She could never escape the cycle until she had the assurance of a love greater than the love she had been seeking in the cycle of sin. God's acceptance is the power that liberates us from sin, not the reward for having liberated ourselves.

That means I don't tell the high school girl who is thinking about losing her virginity, or has lost her virginity, about the dangers of venereal diseases. I don't just tell her what she is doing to her future relationships. There is a place for that, and all those things are true. But most importantly, I tell her that there is a God who cares so much about her, who loves her like a father (maybe a father she's never had), and when she was in danger and she was beyond hope, he pursued her to earth, took upon himself her sin and her shame, took it to a cross, was ripped open for her, and died so that he could wash her, cleanse her, make her new, and make her his precious daughter once again. Why? Because she is never going to have the ability to say no to some guy until she has the assurance of a greater love in Christ. And once she finds and is truly convinced of that love, why would she give herself away to some two-bit guy who just wants to use her for her body?

That means that when I am talking to a man who struggles with pornography, I don't just tell him about what he's doing to his marriage—though I need to tell him that. I also tell him that his Savior went to Calvary to shed his blood for him to make him a man of honor, a man in his image, a man who is respectable.

Jesus put that kind of price on you; therefore, you can live for him and not for yourself. But that man will never have the power to do it until he has the power of a greater acceptance in Christ. That's why Jesus' last words on the cross were, "It is finished," not "Go fix yourself." Because you can only begin to get better, you can only begin to be fixed, when you know that his acceptance of you is not dependant on you fixing yourself or getting better. Only the weightiness of God's acceptance empowers us to forsake idolatry. That's how he breaks the power of canceled sin and sets the prisoner free.

Our message cannot simply be "stop having sex." Our message has to be "behold your God!" One of the most famous examples of a guy caught up in sex is David. For years, I have heard this passage preached as: "Stay off the balcony of your life so you don't see naked Bathsheba running around." The problem is my balcony. How am I going to stay off my balcony? That wasn't the only time David walked out on his balcony. What is really being taught here? Did you ever notice that in the first part of II Samuel 11, David was at home while everyone else was away at battle? In other words, what you see is the image of a king who is disconnected from God's work and God's battle. The answer is not to simply stay off the balcony. You can put a filter on your computer, you can avoid going to lunch with people of the opposite sex, but ultimately there is no way to foolproof your life. There is no way to seal off all the balconies. Bathsheba is there. What you must do is be consumed by God and his work so completely that it breaks the cravings of a soul that longs to go after Bathsheba.

How does that happen? What you must see is that there was a king, another king, who died in your place to free you from the damage of sin. He was the opposite of David. David murdered Uriah to conceal his sin, but Jesus laid down his life to wash away the sins of his people. And you see the beauty of that greater king. That beauty so consumes you that it liberates you from the power of sin. The Puritans used to call this the "expulsive power of a new affection." I love that phrase—it's so Puritan-esque. It means that all the little affections in your life, like sex, are brought into captivity not through self-discipline, but through a greater affection. The problem is not that sexual desires are too strong; the problem is that our sense of the presence of the glory and love of God is so weak.

Tim Chester says this regarding pornography: "Porn is a sin of imagination."[3] We need to counter it by enlarging our imaginations. The answer to porn is to believe the truth. But that is so much more than just an intellectual process. We need to let the truth capture our imaginations—to meditate, ponder, wonder at, and sing the truth. We need to feel the truth, glory in the truth, delight in the truth. The power of new life flows from the cross of Jesus Christ. When Jesus wanted to choose an image for

---

3   Tim Chester, *Closing the Window: Steps to Living Porn Free* (Downers Grove, Ill.: IVP Books, 2010), 64.

salvation, he chose the image of the serpent suspended on the pole and said: You remember that story in the Old Testament where the people were bitten by venomous snakes? They crawled on their hands and knees, and by just looking at this bronze serpent, God's power flowed into them and they got up and were healed. Now, look at the Savior who was crucified and let him heal that sexual dysfunction in your heart, because it's not just a change of perspective—it's an infusion of power. The gospel not only has the power to liberate, it has the power to redeem.

As for the woman in John 4, she becomes Jesus' first witness to the Samaritans. A friend of mine says it like this: First, she came to the well. Then, she met the actual well, the well of living water. Finally, she herself became a well. Some of the greatest disciplers and evangelists in our church are people who have had deep sexual dysfunction in their past. Why? Because that brokenness becomes a well of living water as God's redemption begins to flow out, and we see the multifaceted beauty of the gospel to deal with sexual sin.

4. DON'T AVOID THE HARD TOPICS.

About two years ago our church made a decision—and it was a very difficult decision because our church tries to stay out of politics (we choose not to clutter up our church's platform with things that are important but not necessary to our one mission, to make the gospel clear). Our decision was this: In North Carolina there was an amendment on the ballot that would preserve the legal definition of marriage as being between a man and a woman. Our church is very clear: Marriage is only between a man and a woman, and homosexuality is a deviation from God's plan. It's sinful. But the question was whether we should say anything about this amendment. After a lot of prayer, we made a statement about it. It was a very difficult chapter. Months later, I have no doubts that it was the right decision. God was working through our elder team to have us do that for a number of reasons: The first was to teach our people to think Christianly about the issue. To think Christianly means to reason with grace and truth. Truth without grace is fundamentalism. Grace without truth is sentimentality. Secondly, God uses his Word to bring people to repentance. We had a number of people in the last few months come out of that lifestyle and be saved and baptized.

I would like to conclude with some talking points regarding the issue of same-sex marriage:

A. The point is not homosexuality. The point is the lordship of Jesus. The Bible offends every generation in different ways, and preaching against homosexuality in our day is about as popular as preaching against slavery and racism in Charleston, South Carolina, in 1861. The Bible is an equal opportunity offender. When I lived in a fundamentalist Muslim nation, the story where Jesus forgives the adulteress scandalized them. They would say, "You can't do that! You will unravel the whole institution of marriage if you forgive an adulteress!" Jesus offends. If we are the kind of people who must agree with Jesus to follow him, where is the concept of lordship? Jesus didn't come seeking our votes, he called us to follow.

B. Our stance on this issue may be one of the most important tests of faithfulness in our generation. The courage of a soldier is tested at the place where the battle is the hottest. You don't test a soldier's courage by how well he stands when the battle is no longer being fought. There's no courage involved in that. Courage is shown if you will stand where the battle is being fought. And this issue will test our courage. Are we going to maintain what our culture finds the most offensive?

C. The loss of gender identity has devastating consequences for society. God created us male and female, and when we lose the biblical vision of creation, it skews our vision of God, ourselves, family, and love itself. Wayne Grudem in one of his books cites six different studies—scientific or sociological studies, not Christian in origin. He says that the best thing for a family and the best thing for a society is the union of a man and a woman in a monogamous relationship. There is no question about that at all, statistically speaking.

D. God doesn't send people to hell for homosexuality. You want to know how I know that? Because he doesn't take people to heaven for heterosexuality. He sends people to hell for self-rule and self-righteousness, for thinking they don't need God, that their rules and ways are better than his, and that they can save themselves. That includes the homosexual who rejects God's words for his own. It also includes the self-righteous person who thinks he is fundamentally different or better than the homosexual. It includes the greedy religious person who rejects a life of discipleship to hang on to his riches and reputation. Greed is talked about ten times more than sexual sin. God takes people to heaven for recognizing their sinfulness and falling upon his mercy in repentance and faith. Period.

E. God loves the homosexual. When Jesus said, "Judge not, lest you be judged," he was not saying that we should refuse to declare clearly what God has said clearly. He was saying that our treatment of people who have broken God's laws should be a reflection of how God has treated us. Jesus called out our sin—he didn't mince words—but then he loved us in the midst of it and brought us close. Are we doing the same thing with the homosexual community?

F. We speak as redeemed sinners, not saints. When we understand the gospel we will speak with deep humility, without a drop of hostility or triumphalism. We are not waging a war against homosexuals. Jesus fought and won a war against sin and death *for* homosexuals. They are not the enemy. Sin is the enemy, and Jesus has already defeated it for us. Now we simply testify to his victory and we do so with grace. We do so with love.

G. We can and should be friends with people who are homosexuals. Jesus befriended sinners, starting with us. Thus, we welcome people to our churches and into our lives who are homosexuals. They are made in the image of God. While we cannot stand in Christian fellowship with someone who openly embraces what we believe put Jesus on the cross, something that Jesus calls an abomination; while they can't be members in good standing; while we can't do ministry together, we can love and befriend them. We recognize that many homosexuals are hurting, and many need the touch of grace that Jesus extended to us. We are not waiting for them to make peace with us. That has never been the gospel way. We make peace with them by laying down our lives and going to the stake if we must.

H. Just because you are ticking people off, it doesn't mean you are doing something wrong. John the Baptist got his head cut off for preaching against sexual sin. He told Herod it was not right for him to have another man's wife. Can't you hear the critics and bloggers from our day living in the time of John the Baptist? There is no question what they would have said: "Oh, come on, John! Just stick to love and grace. Preach about Jesus.

There are a lot of people who disagree about this whole marriage thing: Abraham was a polygamist so maybe we shouldn't be preaching like this anyway. Maybe we should just tone it down and focus on the central thing." And can't you see people saying, "John! What a waste. You got your head cut off because you picked on this one guy's sin?" But Jesus said that John was the greatest prophet who ever lived. Today, the spirit of Herod is at work in our world and in our nation. He is still trying to cut off the head of John the Baptist. Is the spirit of John the Baptist at work in us? Just because you are ticking somebody off, it doesn't mean that you are doing something wrong.

I. Avoid pat answers. You know the country preacher who says, "God made woman from a man's rib, and that is why men have one less rib on one side than the other." The same goes for homosexuality. Avoid saying things like, "All homosexuals were abused as kids." Or, "Saved homosexuals become heterosexuals." That's not always true. There are some who live in a constant state of repentance. I have a very good friend in that category. He chose a life of celibacy because those desires and attractions have not really gone away. I have confessed to him before that, even after marrying a drop-dead-gorgeous woman, I seem to have stray sexual desires for other women. That doesn't mean that I acknowledge that I am a polygamist and embrace my impulses. It means that I repent, and I stay faithful to my wife. He says, "I have these desires. They are like your desires that are sinful. I repent of those and I do what God has told me to do."

J. Sexual ethics are not the center of Christianity. The gospel is. The cross and the crown of Jesus are the center. A lesbian girl recently told me, "Here's why I am willing to come to your church, even though I know you disagree with what I say. The university that I go to is only telling me things that they think I want to hear, that they think that I am supposed to hear. Most of the homosexual community that I am a part of knows that the Bible condemns the way that we are living. I know we act like we don't believe that, but we all know it's true. I come to your church because at least you've got the courage to stand up there and say it and not tell me what everybody else is telling me that I should hear. But you also don't single me out, and you don't talk about this as if it's in a fundamentally different category from everybody else's sin. I sense grace there. I don't know if I will ever change my mind, but I will come because I know that I want to be in the presence of God's Word." Sex gets at the core of who we are. Its dysfunction and damage are deep, but the gospel goes deeper still, because where sin abounds, grace abounds more. The great brokenness of sex presents an even greater opportunity for the gospel.

REVIEW QUESTIONS

1. *What is the link between sexual sin and idolatry?*

2. *What can Jesus' encounter with the woman at the well teach us about dealing with sexual brokenness in our own lives and in the lives of those around us?*

3. *How can the sexual confusion in our society lead to opportunities for sharing the gospel?*

═ 4 ═
RESISTING LIPS THAT DRIP HONEY: THE GOSPEL AND MORAL PURITY

JONATHAN AKIN

I grew up in a pastor's home, and there would be nights when my parents would come to us and say they had to go somewhere. They would tell us to put ourselves to bed and get ready for school tomorrow, that they would return. One of those nights was when I was about seventeen years old. It was 10:00 or 10:30 at night, and my parents had to go meet with a couple. And the couple was our good friends.

This was the same couple who sometimes stayed with us when our parents went out of town. The husband was a pastor of a church just outside of town, and they lived about thirty minutes away. On this occasion when my parents had to go to this couple's home, my twin brother and I, being the oldest children, put our brothers to bed. When we returned from school the next day, we asked our parents about the previous night. "Why did you leave so late?" And they told us that our friend, the pastor, was addicted to pornography. His wife had caught him viewing porn and was devastated.

When my parents arrived at the couple's home, the wife was bawling; she could not even speak. At that time, my parents didn't know about the pastor's porn addiction, so my mom suspected he had been unfaithful. But adultery wasn't the problem. Sitting down to talk things through, the pastor revealed he had a porn problem since he was twelve years old. Now he was in his mid-thirties.

When his problem began, he would look at magazines, just occasionally. But with the arrival of the Internet, his problem progressed, until finally he was caught in the grips of this sexual sin. His church was devastated. Should he resign? Should the congregation fire him?

The pastor resigned, entered counseling, and tried to fix his marriage and regain his wife's trust. Fast forward about ten years. He has another pastorate. But one day my father calls and tells me that this same pastor is struggling again. But this time, he's leaving his wife for a lady on his church staff. He was abandoning his wife and family, and he was running off with this other woman. And it was devastating to us because he was such a close friend of our family. What's more, this guy knew the Bible, knew it well, and could preach. But there was an issue that started out when he was twelve, intensified through the years and at age forty-two, had completely destroyed his family, reputation, and ministry.

He had created a god in his own mind, an imaginary, unreal god too gracious to care that his servant was involved in this sin. When caught and confronted, this pastor figured that while he knew this thing was wrong, he could do it anyway because of God's forgiveness. He was walking away from his wife and children, all because of an addiction that began with a lingerie magazine he had seen thirty years earlier.

Many people see no harm in looking at a lingerie magazine. No twelve-year-old thinks forward to age forty-two, when a seeming innocent behavior could become something so monstrous as to completely ruin his ministry and family.

Our friend had this unresolved issue in his heart that progressed in seemingly innocuous and small increments and had become something beyond his control. He had done everything pastors and counselors told him to do to overcome his addiction. He had blocking software on his computer and special software that would send emails to accountability partners. Yes, he joined accountability groups, went to counseling, and allowed Christian men to speak wisdom into his life. He had all of those things, but they didn't work.

When considering wisdom, so many of us think of the book of Proverbs as the Israelite "Dear Abby." We consider Proverbs to just be practical tips for a great life, but that's not what wisdom is, according to the Bible. We think that wisdom is just information transfer, and many sermons have become just that. "Let me give you five principles. Let me give you these three tips. If you will put these things in your life, then it will guard you, then it will you protect you." But that's not the way life works, and that's not the way wisdom works in the Bible. Proverbs teaches us that, fundamentally, wisdom is not a set of facts: Wisdom is personal, Wisdom is a person. In the fullness of time, Scripture reveals that the wisdom of God is Jesus Christ (I Corinthians 1). So wisdom is personal.

Proverbs also tells us that folly is personal, that there are personal beings and spiritual powers at play when it comes to sexuality. These predators are hunting us down, trying to destroy us. And we don't see the hunt; we don't realize we are prey. As a result, we think that if we just learn the proper things and put the right blockers in place, then we'll be safe from harm. But the Bible says, no, we are being hunted down and need the wisdom of God, who is Jesus Christ, for freedom from those things seeking to destroy you.

Consider Proverbs 5:1–6. "My son, be attentive to my wisdom; incline your ear to my understanding, that you may keep discretion, and your lips may guard knowledge. For the lips of a forbidden woman drip honey, and her speech is smoother than oil, but in the end she is bitter as wormwood, sharp as a two-edged sword. Her feet go down to death; her steps follow the path to Sheol; she does not ponder the path of life; her ways wander, and she does not know it."

This passage mentions this woman whose lips drip honey. This is a figure that we see over and over again in Proverbs. I want to give you a gospel-centered strategy for resisting honey lips. We need to be aware of how honey lips attack us, the assault weapons the enemy uses to track us down.

Solomon talks repeatedly about this woman. She is a major character in the book of Proverbs in chapters 2, 5, 6, and 7, and later in the book. He talks repeatedly about her, and he is warning his son: Hey, there's this woman who wants to seduce you and drag you down to the grave, drag you down to Sheol. Now, "she" stands for a real woman with whom Solomon's son might be tempted to commit sexual sin. More significantly, Solomon is using the feminine pronoun to reference sexual sin. Sexual sin is any sex that deviates from the biblical pattern of a man and a woman in a heterosexual, monogamous, lifelong marriage. Any deviation from that is real sexual sin that can destroy us. Some people get bent out of shape because Solomon uses the feminine pronoun to refer to sexual sin. Some say Solomon must have been sexist, presenting a woman as this tiger, or perhaps a cougar, seeking to destroy a young man. To be clear, Proverbs is not Solomon being sexist. It is a father talking to his son. Had Solomon been talking to his daughter, he would have said to look out for the immoral man because, trust me, there are those out there as well.

This book is not written just for the son but for the youth of the nation, both men and women. Women need to read it and realize they can fall prey to sexual sin, as well. If Solomon needed an illustration today, he would probably choose the song "Maneater," right? "Watch out here she comes. She'll chew you up," all these things. "She's a maneater." Were he talking to his daughter today, he might choose Carrie Underwood's "Cowboy Casanova." Or there is this one: My wife's from Knoxville, and the most famous country music star from Knoxville is a guy named Kenny Chesney, and he sings a song called "Out Last Night." And it's amazing to me that Chesney is so brazen in the way that he talks about his romantic pursuits. He talks about all of the different roles he has played to get women to sleep with him. He sings, "I was a doctor and a lawyer and a senator's son, anything I had to be to get the job done." So both men and women can be manipulative in such matters. I advise you to apply the scripture to your own life.

Solomon was not saying that his son was just some innocent bystander in the matter. Solomon explains in chapter 7, and in other places, that his son is not fleeing from sexual sin. He is going near her house; it's at night, when he shouldn't be there. It's the wrong place at the wrong time. He's not an innocent bystander.

When I was growing up in Louisville, Kentucky, a kid in our youth group was on a top-ranked basketball team. They would play in tournaments all over the place at a time when high school students could bypass college for the NBA. At these tournaments, there would be young teenage girls who would travel the tournament circuit and try to sleep with the players. These girls hoped to get pregnant and use the child as a meal ticket when the father was drafted by an NBA team.

There was a guy on this team who was not really good; he was being recruited by some Division II schools. But he would tell these girls he was highly recruited, going straight from high school to the NBA with a million-dollar contract, just to get these girls to sleep with him. They were preying on him, but he was preying on them. Nobody is innocent in this. Everybody is involved in this sexual sin. Solomon is not trying to present his son as an innocent bystander facing destruction from a woman. Instead, Solomon is trying to warn him about the way these things work. And yes, there's this real woman who can go after him and lure him into sexual sin.

Proverbs also tells us, again, that we are not only faced with the fact that wisdom is a person with whom we can have a relationship, but that folly is personal as well. The whole of Proverbs 1–9 is Solomon trying to get his son to be in a personal relationship with wisdom, presented as a woman, instead of a personal relationship with foolishness, also presented as a woman. That's the hope. For the son to walk in the wisdom of Proverbs 10–31 and all of the wise sayings in Proverbs 10–31, he has to choose to embrace the woman wisdom, instead of the woman folly. Solomon uses a poetic device called personification when he presents wisdom and folly as women. He takes something that is an abstract idea and gives it lifelike qualities. We might talk about the flag, as in "these colors don't run," or say that "lady justice is blind." It's personification. Solomon is personifying the wisdom of God as an attractive woman. Solomon uses a feminine pronoun because the word for wisdom in Hebrew is a female noun; in personification, the personification would take on the gender of the word personified. Also, this is a dad talking to his son. If you want to get your son's attention, presenting an attractive woman to him will get his attention. That is going to be much more intriguing than saying, "Hey, sit down, let me tell you some facts about wisdom. Let's talk about these things."

This personification of wisdom is later revealed to be embodied. Jesus is the embodiment of the wisdom of God, as referenced in I Corinthians 1.

Solomon also personified foolishness as a woman, and the exact same things are said about her in Proverbs 9 that are said about this immoral woman in Proverbs 5 and 7. She is going to lure you with her words. She is going to drag you down to death, to the grave. And she lives in a palace at the top of the city, which in the ancient world would be a temple. In Proverbs, folly stands for idols, false gods. Ultimately, I think, in New Testament terms, we could say this stands for the god of this age, who is Satan.

This is why Paul gives us some of the very same wisdom in I Corinthians 6 and 7 that Solomon is giving us here in Proverbs 5. What Paul says in I Corinthians 7 is that if you are not engaged in regular intimacy with your wife, then you are giving Satan room to tempt you and attack you. That is exactly what's happening in Proverbs. Folly is a personal predator coming after you to destroy and kill you with sexual sin as a weapon.

Beginning in Proverbs 7:21, Solomon uses the imagery of an ox going to the slaughter, of a stag being caught fast until an arrow pierces its liver, of a bird rushing into a trap. The one captured does not know the trap will cost him his life. Solomon talks about a hunt, somebody seeking to kill the prey.

Proverbs 23:26 says, "My son, give me your heart, and let your eyes observe my ways. For a prostitute is a deep pit; an adulteress is a narrow well. She lies in wait like a robber and increases the traitors among mankind." Again it's like a predator that wants to track you down, that wants to trap and kill you. And that's what foolishness is. That's what Satan is trying to do. There are personal beings at play that want to offer whatever will entice you, to entrap you and then blow you away. That's exactly what foolishness is doing in the area of sexual sin.

There are two main weapons folly uses to entrap you. The first—the first and most prominent one in the book of Proverbs—is communication. We think attraction is where unfaithfulness to our spouse starts, but in Proverbs, Solomon mainly warns his son about communication. "The lips of a forbidden woman drip honey." And that is not just saying she tastes sweet to kiss, although that imagery is used. Solomon, in fact, uses it in Song of Solomon to talk about his wife, so there's probably a double entendre here in Proverbs. But Solomon is mainly talking about the second thing he mentions—her speech is smoother than oil. He is talking about her words. She uses alluring words to drag you into sexual sin that will bring you down to death.

It shouldn't surprise us, especially us men, that communication is where unfaithfulness starts, because men are suckers for flattery. Our egos are easily inflated. We like to read our press clippings, and we like to believe it when people pat us pastors on the back and say we preached a great sermon. "Pastor, I have never heard anyone preach on that topic like you did. Nobody has every opened my eyes to the Scriptures like that." And you are thinking, "Yeah, it's because I'm just such a biblically-minded, wonderful preacher." It's just easy for us to have our egos inflated. And also, think about women in the same situation as us. Women, in terms of intimacy, desire communication. For both the man and the woman, flattery presents a challenge. This is a way for people to be drawn into sexual temptation and sexual immorality.

There are people in your church that you are ministering to, discipling, and preaching to who will do things that they never dreamed they would do, things that will cause their children to never forgive them, and it will start with seemingly innocent communication. It will start with such ideas as: "She is fun to talk to at work, and she seems to like my jokes a little bit better than my wife, and she seems to be a little bit easier to talk to than my wife." For a lady, it may begin when she believes her coworker is a much better listener than her husband: "He really listens to me. He's not just thinking about the next thing that he is going to say. He actually gets what I'm talking about, and I can have an actual conversation with him." For a man, it might start with getting a friend request from an old girlfriend and beginning to wonder what she's up to: "What's the big deal if I'm friends with her? Maybe we can kind of catch up from time to time." I'm not saying you should never talk to somebody of the opposite sex. But when you become discontent in your relationship with your spouse, you may begin to look forward to work because a seemingly fun, playful flirtation is waiting there. Well then, you should just hear the *Jaws* music in the back of your brain because you are being hunted. Five months or five years later, you will look back and wonder how in the world you got to this place that ruined your marriage and family. And it started all the way back here because you weren't paying attention, when you behaved like an ox grazing the field that ends up at the slaughterhouse.

It starts with communication. If you are regularly texting with, emailing, Facebook messaging, or whatever to somebody of the opposite sex because it makes you feel happy, important, or fulfilled, that's really dangerous. Such communication breeds discontentment with your wife, it breeds discontentment with your husband, and it is extremely dangerous. That's where a lot of unfaithfulness starts. This communication can lure you into sexual sin.

There's also communication by folly itself, by the god of this age, by the culture that's downloading messages into your brain about sexuality that are going to cause you to think wrong things about sex. Such messages claim infidelity is much hotter, much more pleasurable than monogamy. The culture says, "Don't get married so young, just fool around with your girlfriend; it's no big deal." Culture asks, "How are you going to know what you like if you don't do those kinds of things?" And people begin to believe these false messages; people get drawn into infidelity and sexual sin through communication.

In addition to communication, folly uses a second weapon, attraction. This obviously can take the form of pornography, but it can also materialize in movies, or just in mundane, everyday life. I enjoy going to Opry Mills in Nashville and while my wife shops for forty-five minutes in Carter's, I sit and engage in people watching. I don't know why I like to do this; I guess because I am a fundamentalist pastor at heart, I like to watch men's behavior as women walk by. Part of my interest is because I want to make sure I am not doing the same thing these men do. They're not even subtle about this at all, the way their eyes follow the women. If your sons and your daughters see you eyeing women passing by, what are you teaching them? It can pull your heart. You may think it's not a big deal, but looking leads to fantasies in the mind and discontentment. In a culture that is trying to define beauty and attractiveness for us, we need to establish our wife as our personal standard of beauty. Beauty is not some external category in relation to my wife. There is not this ideal of beauty by which my wife must be measured. No, Ashley Akin is my standard of beauty. And the way Ashley Akin looks is beautiful. There is no external category. So, when Ashley Akin is nine months pregnant, beauty for me is a nine-month-fully-pregnant, blond haired woman. Many guys fall into this trap and allow an external standard of beauty to damage their marriage. They discourage their wives from eating that doughnut. Or, they insist she should get on the treadmill. Such an approach demeans their wife and their marriage, because they view attraction as something outside of their wife. No, your wife is your standard of beauty, and you shouldn't be training yourself to see other women as beautiful in that kind of way, in a sexual kind of a way.

Early in my pastorate, I encountered members who would take their ten- or eleven-year-old son to Hooters and have his picture taken with the waitresses hugging and kissing the child. They thought it was cute; I thought it was stupid! I remember counseling a couple who had suffered the husband's infidelity. I discovered they liked to watch porn to add spice to their marriage. I questioned why they would do that. She was training her husband to find another woman attractive and sexually stimulating, and then she was surprised that he cheated on her. Attraction is the second weapon that will lead us down the path to death.

We need to be warned about the consequences of sexual sin, both temporal and eternal consequences. We see in Proverbs 5 that folly is going to kill you. The predator is going to track you down and kill you. This death will include some really nasty temporary consequences, and then some ultimate consequences. Temporary consequences are stated in Proverbs 5, beginning in verse 7. Solomon says, "And now, O sons, listen to me, and do not depart from the words of my mouth. Keep your way far from her, and do not go near the door of her house, lest you give your honor to others and your years to the merciless, lest strangers take their fill of your strength, and your labors go to the house of a foreigner, and at the end of your life you groan, when your flesh and body are consumed, and you say, 'How I hated discipline, and my heart despised reproof! I did not listen to the voice of my teachers or incline my ear to my instructors. I am at the brink of utter ruin in the assembled congregation.'"

The bottom line, Solomon says, is if you fall into sexual sin, all of the labor you've invested in your marriage will go to someone else. When it comes to your marriage, you are going to labor. Just think about it. Think about the amount of man-hours you put into pursuing your wife, marrying your wife, cultivating your relationship with your wife. Think about the man-hours you've put into your children, cultivating a relationship with them. Think of the man-hours and labor you have put into your family. If you fall into sexual sin, Solomon says, someone else is going to enjoy the fruit of your labor.

This is exactly the warning God gives the children of Israel about being unfaithful to him. When he tells them about blessing in the book of Deuteronomy, he tells them they will enjoy something for which they didn't labor. And the curses that are laid out in Deuteronomy entail your labors benefitting someone else. You planted vineyards, you dug wells, you built houses, and somebody else is going to live in them; somebody else is going to drink from your wells; somebody else is going to eat your crops. And that is exactly what Solomon is saying in terms of your family.

There is a country song that came out a couple of years ago that is really heartbreaking, but it paints this picture. It's by Toby Keith, and he sings about driving through town and passing by his house, his car, his dog in the backyard, his kids, and his wife. But he asks "Who is that man who is running my life?" His ex-wife is now married to somebody else, whom his kids are now calling Dad. And Solomon says: Listen, if you mess up in this area, if you fall in this area, somebody else is going to kiss your wife goodnight, your kids are going to call somebody else Dad, and all those things for which you labored will go to somebody else.

Solomon goes on to say that sickness can come from this folly, and we could go into STDs and the like. In verse 11, he warns that "your body and your flesh are consumed." In verse 12, Solomon mentions regret: "You say, 'How I hated discipline and my heart despised reproof. I did not listen to the voice of my teachers or incline my ear to my instructors.'" There's regret over the opportunities that you had to repent and see the foolishness that was going on in your life, and you refused it. One thing that really ticks me off about men is when their wives lovingly warn them about they way they're relating to a woman, and the men will make their wives feel like idiots for cautioning them. They will belittle and intimidate their wife, questioning her motives while proclaiming that nothing is amiss. Whoever treats their wife in this fashion is a moron. A man should see this as the goodness of God, calling the husband to be aware of the things that might lead to destruction. And so, Solomon speaks of a man's regret for not having heeded his wife's warning. A husband should receive such a warning as the goodness of God calling the sinner to repentance.

And then the sinner's reputation is gone: "I'm at the brink of utter ruin in the assembled congregation." Solomon is referring to church discipline as a result of this sexual sin. In chapter 6, Solomon says the spurned husband will seek revenge against you. We see that there are many kinds of negative consequences.

At age twenty-five, when I had been a pastor for about a month, a man asked to come see me. Among the pastors of our church at the time was Jimmy Scroggins, who, having more experience, sat in on the meeting. This man confessed to us that he was having an affair. He had met a woman in a chat room, whose son played on a soccer team with his son. They started the affair, and while they hadn't been caught, he felt guilty and ashamed. We told him to confess to his wife, which he did not feel confident to do. We advised him that if he didn't confess, she would likely find out, and he could lose any chance at saving his marriage. He resisted, saying nobody else knew, that there was no way she could find out, and that he just wasn't ready to confess.

Instead of confessing, he decided to continue the discussion after the family vacation in Myrtle Beach. On their return drive to Louisville after the vacation, his wife got a phone call from the ex-husband of the woman the man was having this affair with. The ex-husband said that he wanted her to know what her husband had been doing. They had eight hours left on the drive—in the same car, of course, with the kids in the back seat. There are all kinds of temporal consequences that will happen if you fall in this area, and you need to be warned. But we also need to be warned about the eternal consequences.

In Proverbs 22:14, Solomon says, "The mouth of forbidden women is a deep pit; he with whom the LORD is angry will fall into it." Now, here's the thing we often think to ourselves: If I do these things, then God will get angry with me and zap me. He will teach me my lesson. Solomon is saying the fact that you have already fallen is a sign that God is already judging you, not that he is going to judge you in the future. He is already judging you. He has removed his restraining hand, and he has given you over to your fleshly desires, as Paul referenced in Romans 1. The fact that you have had to erase the Internet history on your computer once again is a sign that God is judging you right now, and you loathe yourself because of it. Solomon says: You have fallen into this pit, and it is a sign that God has turned you over to your own evil passions. Proverbs 5:21 says that the Lord sees our ways. He sees what we are doing in this area. Nothing you do goes unnoticed, and you will be held to account for it. Proverbs is clear about this. Often we consider the consequences of sexual sin: that we may lose our family, lose our children's respect, lose our money, contract some kind of sickness, lose our ministry and church. All of those consequences are possible. But even if those things don't happen to you, you will still be held accountable for what you have done. And if those things do happen to you, then it's just a foretaste of the judgment that is to come. Proverbs is clear about this. When you reap what you sow immediately in temporary consequences, that's just a foretaste of the judgment that is going to come.

And so, we need to not just talk about the temporal consequences of sexual sin, but we also need to talk about the eternal consequence, which is that you are going to hell. The wages of sexual sin is death. Don't you know that the sexually immoral will not inherit the kingdom of God? We need to talk about hell when it comes to sexual sin, because Jesus talked about hell as a consequence of sexual sin. Gouge out your eye instead of going to hell. And we need to think in that way. We need to think in those terms. Internet blockers and other barriers are not effective if they are your only defense. But that doesn't mean that you should do less than that. You should do whatever it takes to fight this in your life, even if it means that you get rid of your smart phone and get a flip phone that doesn't include the Internet. Here's the image Proverbs is using, and we need to be clear about this: If there were a sexual predator loose in your house, what would you do to protect yourself and family? You would blow his head off, right? Well, why would we allow a predator to be loose in our house and just say, "Well, you know, I am going to put up a little baby gate to keep the predator out from my family and me." No, Jesus said gouge out your eye. Cut off your hand. Do whatever you have to do to fight this. And if that means zero access to the Internet, that means zero access to the Internet. That means you are never alone with a woman, you don't take a member of the opposite sex to lunch, or you don't go into a house to counsel a woman alone. This is not because women are evil or malicious, this is because men know their own hearts. Jesus seemed to say "go overboard" in Matthew 5. The warnings that God gives to us—we're meant to heed them so that we may walk in a path of purity and avoid destruction.

But these measures are not enough in and of themselves. You need to embrace the gospel. Proverbs is clear that wisdom is, first of all, about a right relationship with God, a right vertical relationship that leads to right horizontal relationship. In the beginning, when God created the world, there was harmony between man and God. When Eve and Adam foolishly ate the fruit, it broke their relationship with God, so they hid from God. They thought eating the fruit would make them wise, but it broke their relationships with each other and stole the intimacy they once enjoyed. That tie between our vertical relationship with God and our horizontal relationship with our spouse is correlated over and over again in the Bible, such that Israel's idolatry is called adultery, playing the whore, playing the prostitute, playing the harlot. It's repeated over and over again. Solomon knows this full well. Solomon knew that sexual sin pulled his heart away from God and led him to worship idols. Your vertical relationship with God is directly correlated with your horizontal relationship with your spouse, and if one is off, the other is going to be off. Proverbs teaches us that if we embrace the wisdom of God, who is Jesus

Christ, if we embrace him and fear the Lord, it will lead to a right relationship with our spouse.

Solomon warns his son throughout chapters 1–9 about foolishness, encouraging him to embrace wisdom. The only way to walk in wisdom and purity is to have this personal relationship with Jesus. Furthermore, we learn in Proverbs 10–31 that if you fall short of the wisdom God has revealed, then you have a problem with Jesus. If you are not able to be faithful to your spouse, if you are constantly fantasizing about somebody else, or constantly looking at pornography, or constantly flirting with somebody else, then you are not only a bad husband, but you also have a problem with Jesus. You are not rightly believing the gospel. You have some idolatry in your life that is causing this kind of issue in your life.

We need to return to constantly preaching the gospel to ourselves and equipping our people to preach the gospel to themselves, because here's the deal: Long before Jesus Christ came to the earth; went to the cross; crushed the head of the predator; died for his bride, the church; freed her from sin; and developed a covenant one-flesh union with his bride, God gave us a picture of the gospel when he gave us marriage. That's what Paul says in Ephesians 5. In marriages we are to replay the intimate, pure, sacrificial, other-seeking love that Christ has for his bride. We are to replay that gospel message in our marriages. And what happens is that when we deviate from that in our marriages—whether it's pornography, cohabitation, fornication, adultery, or homosexuality—we are lying about the gospel. We are mocking the gospel and being turned on by that mockery of the gospel because we fail to believe it. We fail to believe it. The gospel is what is going to free us in this area of our lives.

Preach the gospel to yourself every day. That means you need to remind yourself of the continual need to repent of sin. What I mean by that is this: There is not one of us who has graduated the class of sexual purity to the point that it is not going to be an issue for us anymore. And if you think you have, take heed lest you fall. We need to constantly remind ourselves that we are not going to arrive at this until Jesus comes to get us or we go to be with him. Until then, there is going to be a need for continual repentance in the Christian life.

We need to remind ourselves of Romans 6: "How can we who have died to sin continue to live in it?" The power of the resurrection is at work in your life, so you have the power to fight this. Now, I am not saying that you are going to necessarily achieve complete perfection and rid yourself of all of these sexual temptations in your life, areas where you are prone to fall and sin. What I am saying is this: You have, by the Spirit of Christ living in you and the power of the resurrection, the ability to fight this sin, an ability you didn't have before. Don't give up the fight. Don't lay down the sword and accept defeat as who you are, which is what a lot of people in our culture do. Don't do that.

We need to remind ourselves that we are forgiven, that we are not condemned. In II Peter 1, Peter reminds us we are not progressing in the Christian life because we have forgotten that we have been cleansed of our former sins. So preach the gospel to yourself. Train your congregation to preach the gospel to themselves every morning, not just the gospel vertically but the gospel horizontally. We must realize the beauty of the gospel message as revealed in heterosexual marriage. That is what Solomon says in Proverbs 5: "Drink water from your own cistern, flowing water from your own well. Should your springs be scattered abroad, streams of water in the streets? Let them be for yourself alone, and not for strangers with you. Let your fountain be blessed, and rejoice in the wife of your youth, a lovely deer, a graceful doe. Let her breasts fill you at all times with delight; be intoxicated always in her love. Why should you be intoxicated, my son, with a forbidden woman and embrace the bosom of an adulteress?"

Pursue your wife. This is exactly what Paul says in I Corinthians 6 when he says to flee sexual immorality. He says to have a conjugal relationship with your wife, which in many ways is the antidote to adultery.

Trevor Longman wrote a great commentary on the book of Proverbs. He says the best defense against sexual sin is a strong offense in marriage. I love that quote, and I write it on the mirror of my bathroom and let my wife read it. I'm just kidding—I don't do that. The best defense against sexual sin is a strong offense in marriage. That's not just true for the people in your congregation that are married right now; that's also true for the children and the teenagers in your congregation. You have to point them to the beauty of marriage and teach them that these sexual urges and sexual feelings are not bad. Here is a very specific prescription: you were meant to be married. And so preach the gospel vertically, and preach it horizontally in our marriages.

Lastly, the warning of Proverbs is that if you fall in this area—and all of us have fallen in this area—you are going to be dragged down to the pit and you are never going to come back. The good news of the gospel is that Jesus is not just the wisdom of the book of Proverbs; he's also the son in the book of Proverbs who went into the pit for your sexual sin, crushed the head of the predator, and came back alive. And if you are in him, joined to him by faith, there is no condemnation for you. The power of the resurrection is at work in your life, freeing you from these things. Rest in that good news, and rest in the picture of that good news that is your marriage.

REVIEW QUESTIONS

1. *How can we cultivate wisdom by avoiding sexual temptation in our lives?*

2. *In what ways are we wrongly believing the gospel if we indulge in sexual sin?*

3. *How can we "preach the gospel to ourselves"? What does this look like in our everyday lives?*

= 5 =
THE BIRDS AND THE BEES: THE GOSPEL AND YOUR CHILDREN'S SEXUALITY

DAVID PRINCE

Using I Corinthians 6 as a guide, I want to discuss how we can teach our children a gospel-centered, biblical understanding of sexuality. First Corinthians 6:19–20 says: "Or do you not know that your body is a temple of the Holy Spirit within you, whom you have from God? You are not your own, for you were bought with a price. So glorify God in your body."

I am a child of the 1980s. One of the best things about the eighties—besides having the best music—is that there were no personal computers and no iPhones. I want you to flash back with me for a moment to the eighties. I want you to picture a father who walks in his son's room, and he spreads pornographic magazines all around the edges of the room. His son looks at him and says, "What's that, Dad?"

His father replies, "I don't want to talk about it. I just want you to know two things. The first thing is: do not look at those magazines. The second thing is: don't do what's inside those magazines because if you do, you might not get the things that you want in life. You might mess up your desire to go to college, your desire to have a career. You might not have as bright and as successful a future ahead of you."

That would be bad parenting. In fact, it is the worst approach possible in every single aspect. First of all it, creates in the child's life an access to pornography and with that a corrupt vision and view of sexuality. Not only does it create that access and that corrupt view—it doesn't provide a positive framework to understand and process issues related to sexuality. And finally, the appeal, the motive for certain moral and ethical behavior is purely an appeal for self-interest. Is that not largely the approach of many Christian parents in our churches today, except that it's far worse, isn't it? It's one thing to have a magazine in an isolated spot in your home. It's another thing to have a twenty-four-hour-a-day sex show available to you at all times. If your children have unmonitored access to the Internet, you are a negligent parent.

Sexual liberationists teach that sex is all about self-fulfillment and self-expression. They understand sex and sexuality abstracted from God, abstracted from the gospel. But here's the problem: Even though we criticize the sexual liberationists for abstracting sexuality from God, a lot of evangelical parents refuse to teach their children about sexuality. "Don't do that. Just say no." When parents do that, they are abstracting the issue of sexuality from the gospel. Sex is all about the gospel. Marriage is all about the gospel.

We have sort of a Pharisaical-Sadducean theology when it comes to teaching our children about sex. The Pharisaical aspect of it is this: The Pharisees looked at the Scriptures as a moral law code. You define yourself by the things you don't do: "We are the people who don't do that." And so we look at our children, and we say, "Do not have sex before marriage." But that's all we say. We tend to appeal to them on the basis of living a good life, a successful life, a life that is marked by comfort. We don't know a lot about the Sadducees, but they do seem to be a sort of aristocratic class who wanted to defend the status quo. They only held to the authority of the first five books of the Bible. They rejected a lot of things, because they didn't want a revolution. Life was too good. And they wanted good kids. And so, if we talk to our children about issues of sexuality, and all we say is: "Don't have sex. Don't have sex before marriage, and don't think about getting married until you are older, because after all, don't you want a good life? If you are saddled with a wife and child at an early age, you might not go to college. You might not get a degree." There's a biblical term for that approach. You know what it is? It's worldliness.

Worldliness is not a word that we use a lot today, and that is partly good, because the way that we've come to hear the term doesn't have anything to do with the way that Paul is using it in I and II Corinthians. We tend to think that worldliness is about morality. There is a right behavior, and people who have the right behavior are the good guys. There is a wrong behavior, and people who have the wrong behavior are the bad guys. And so we position issues related to morality in terms of tribal identity. And if we are the good guys who don't do certain things, then we seem to have an attitude of superiority, as though we are inherently morally superior to other people. And those who are the bad guys are morally inferior to other people. This sort of tribal identity doesn't do anything to speak to the truth of the gospel.

In I and II Corinthians, Paul is dealing with divisiveness in the church. In I Corinthians he is primarily dealing with issues within the context of the church, and in II Corinthians he is primarily dealing with issues of divisiveness in relation to his apostolic ministry. But both situations are the same. There are those people who say, "I am spiritual because I have this gift or ability. I am spiritual because I do these things or am part of this group." Their identity is bound up in their gifts, their ability, or their expertise. And Paul is saying, no, the believer in Jesus Christ is not inherently morally superior. In fact, he's a sinner who needs the grace of God. The dividing line between worldliness and the word of the cross is not inherent moral superiority. It is a crucified Christ. When we define the world in terms of the good guys and bad guys, it has nothing to do with the gospel or reaching people for the gospel of Jesus Christ.

A lot of the ways we train our children to think about the world has a lot more to do with what Paul describes as "worldly wisdom" than it does the word of the cross, which is the wisdom of God. When Paul says in I Corinthians 2:2, "I am determined to know nothing among you but Christ and him crucified," he means that the lens by which he views the world is in light of Jesus Christ crucified. It's in light of the cross, meaning not that he is a dead savior, but he was crucified as the Savior. He rose from the dead. He is establishing his kingdom. Paul says that if you embrace the word of the cross, if you embrace the wisdom of God, it means that you think about the world in light of redemptive history, which centers on the person of Jesus Christ. You want to know everything in light of that story, and you define your life in light of that story, which ends in the consummation of the kingdom in a new heaven and a new earth. Worldliness, he says defines the world based on self-interest, living for the moment, our gifts and abilities, and our observable successes. It says that my identity is bound up in my achievements and self-satisfaction. When you do that, that is worldly wisdom. You can do that with conservative morality or liberal morality. If you define the world by saying, "I know I'm a good person because I've never been involved in fornication, because I always go to church, because I am not involved"—that is worldliness.

Worldliness comes in a conservative moral package as well as a liberal morality package. Worldliness is evaluating the world without the cross at the center. We define what is good for ourselves, and then we call Jesus to help us establish our good. In other words, instead of bowing before Christ and his kingdom, we want to build a kingdom and hire Jesus as our subcontractor. Paul calls that attitude worldliness. First Corinthians 6 is often treated as though it's a section of Scripture that is unrelated. The first eight verses deal with lawsuits, verses 9 through 11 deal with issues of lifestyle behavior, and the remainder deals specifically with the issue of appetites. In reality, this entire section is talking about the same thing. There's a connection between all these sections.

First Corinthians 6:2 says, "Or do you not know?" Verse three, "Or do you not know?" Verse nine, "Or do you not know?" And then if you skip down to verse 15, "Or do you not know?" Verse 16, "Or do you not know?" Verse 19, "Or do you not know?" Paul is making the same case in all of these sections. The first section deals with lawsuits: the corrupt Roman process in the civil courts. Whoever had the most power to offer a bribe, whoever had the most position of authority to leverage their authority could get their way in the court system. Verse one says, "Does he dare to go to the law before the unrighteous instead of the saints?" You are suing one another, and the reason you are doing it is because you can leverage your position of authority to get what you want. What's the problem with that? The problem with that is that the crucified Messiah did not use his authority for his own advantage but for the advantage of others.

In verse seven, Paul argues, "To have lawsuits at all with one another is already a defeat for you. Why not rather suffer wrong? Why not rather be defrauded?" The first section is about power, but it is power understood through the lens of a cross. It's power understood through the lens of a crucified Messiah. When you look at the cross, you see infinite power being given in self-sacrifice for undeserving sinners. The distinctive power that he's calling believers to is the power to be wronged, the power to be deprived, the power to be self-sacrificial for a greater good—the good of Christ and his kingdom.

"Or do you not know that the unrighteous will not inherit the kingdom of God?" (1 Corinthians 6:9) The passage is talking about the kingdom, Christ crucified and his kingdom. And then it talks about lifestyle behaviors. "Do not be deceived: neither the sexually immoral, nor idolaters, nor adulterers, nor men who practice homosexuality, nor thieves, nor the greedy, nor drunkards, nor revilers, nor swindlers will inherit the kingdom of God." Paul is talking here about habitual behavior. He's not talking about struggles at a given time. He's talking about giving yourself over to the habitual activity. What they all have in common is the idea that I have to step away from what God has said, and I have to do what feels right to me. In verse 11 he says, "And such were some of you. But you were washed, but you were sanctified, but you were justified in the name of the Lord Jesus Christ and by the Spirit of our God." God is at work in the world saving sinners, not cleaning up the righteous. He is at work saving sinners. "Such were some of you," but now you are a new creation in Christ Jesus.

The last section deals with food and the body. Paul has no sympathy with the view that we separate our spirituality from our physicality. There is a wholeness to the work of the gospel. God has a future for our bodies. Verse 13 says, "The body is not meant for sexual immorality, but for the Lord, and the Lord for the body." Verse 14: "And God raised the Lord and will also raise us up by his power. Do you not know that your bodies are members of Christ? Shall I then take the members of Christ and make them members of a prostitute? Never! Or do you not know that he who is joined to a prostitute becomes one body with her? For, as it is written, 'The two will become one flesh.' But he who is joined to the Lord becomes one spirit with him. Flee from sexual immorality. Every other sin a person commits is outside the body, but the sexually immoral person sins against his own body. You are not your own, for you were bought with a price. Glorify God in your body." You have been bought and paid for in Jesus Christ.

Leon Morris says in his commentary on these verses, "We are probably witnessing here the first attempt in the history of moral thought to refute libertinism in some other way than by arguments of legalism. The motive is not self-fulfillment. The motive is God's glory in Christ." This is not Pharisaical. We do not define ourselves by what we don't do and trust in that. It's not Sadducean. We do not define ourself as the good people and defend the status quo. But rather it is the radical reality that we are to see every category in our lives, every thought in our lives transformed by the cross. We are to have a cruciform view of the world. In II Corinthians, Paul is dealing with these super apostles who are saying, "He's weak. He doesn't speak well. He doesn't have the right credentials. He's worldly." Paul refutes them, and he says this at the end of the section in II Corinthians 12: "I fear that when I come again my God may humble me before you, and I may have to mourn over many of those who sinned earlier and have not repented of the impurity, sexual immorality, and sensuality that they have practiced."

Here's what I want you to see: We must have a distinctive, Christ-centered understanding of everything—including sexuality. We are to understand sexuality in light of redemptive history, in light of Jesus' crucifixion, and in light of the promise of the eschatological kingdom of Christ. Without gospel-centered eschatology there are no sexual ethics. There are just special interest groups for this morality or that morality. There's no such thing as a definable sexual ethic or any other ethic. Moralism and legalism are failures. You can't feed the flesh to kill it. It doesn't matter whether the morality is abstracted from the gospel to the left or the right. Understanding morality abstracted from the gospel and seeing yourself defined by that has no power because either way it feeds the flesh.

We cannot allow the world to frame the discussion about sexuality that we need to have with our children. You've got to define the issue, top to bottom, in light of Jesus Christ and the gospel. Let me put it to you this way: If you want good kids, that's a problem. We don't want good kids, we want gospel kids. We don't want nice kids—we want kids who are radical about the gospel of Jesus Christ, and so sexuality is one of those primary ways in which we teach them about the reality of the gospel. This means that our approach to teaching our children about Christian sexuality cannot be "no, just don't do it." That is not a Christian sexual ethic. We can't just say "be good kids, be good people." That is not Christian sexuality. We want them not to just have a right view about what to say no to—we want them to have a comprehensively Christ-centered, Christian view of sexuality.

A comprehensive Christian view of sexuality is about delight. It's not just what we say no to—it's what we say yes to. Here are eight gospel trajectories in thinking about how to deal with your children in relation to cultivating an understanding of Christian sexuality:

1. UNDERSTAND SEX EDUCATION AS A VITAL COMPONENT OF A GOSPEL EDUCATION.

Genesis 1:27–28 tells us that God created image bearers. He created them male and female. He told them to be fruitful and multiply and fill the earth and subdue it. The issue of marriage and the issue of sexual intercourse in the context of marriage, the marital act, is a part of the natural created order. The Bible tells us it points beyond the natural created order to something else. Genesis 2:24 says, "Therefore a man shall leave his father and his mother and hold fast to his wife and they shall become one flesh." Ephesians 5 is about Christ and the church, of which marriage is a picture. Christ and the church are primary; marriage is the reflection. So, in the very beginning we see that God gave the institution of marriage and sexual activity in the context of marriage to point beyond itself to the glory and mystery of the gospel of Jesus Christ, the relationship between Christ and the church. So, when we deal with our children, we must teach them about sexual activity because it's a part of teaching them about the gospel. This is an image that God has given.

2. TEACH YOUR CHILDREN THAT SEX IS WHAT YOU ARE—NOT WHAT YOU HAVE.

Anthony Esolen puts it like this:

> The very word sex derives from the Latin word *sexus*, denoting that which separates. It is cognate with a whole host of words for severance such as schism, scissors, sect. It is a mark of our degeneracy that the very term "having sex" has come to mean the marital act when once the delicate term "making love" similarly denoted. What a man and woman do in the marriage bed is not have sex. The sex that is the separation they are provided already. What they do is unite across the separation in the marital act.[1]

That means that we teach them about sex and sexual intercourse, beginning with the fact that we are gendered image-bearers. A part of what God does to image himself in the world is that he has made us male and female. If we are going to

---

1   Anthony Esolen, "Sanity & Matrimony: Ten Arguments in Defense of Marriage," *Touchstone*, July/August 2010.

effectively image him we have to embrace what God has given. We have to celebrate our gendered identity. We ought to do that with our children and cultivate an environment of thankfulness for our gender identity—not a situation in which we want to blur those distinctions. The way we image God in the world is the fact that he has given us an identity: male and female.

One of the ways we try to do this in our home is how my wife and I interact with one another—in a way that is thankful for the roles that God has given us as a husband and a wife. Another way we do it is by praying for them. When I pray for my sons and daughters, I thank God for making them the gender they are. I ask that God help each of them understand what it means to have their masculinity or femininity surrendered to Christ. You see, it is clarity about sexual identity and thankfulness to the God who made us gendered image-bearers that are foundational to teaching them a proper attitude toward sexual intercourse and sex in the context of marriage.

Another factor that is often overlooked is the way brothers and sisters relate to one another. They are learning how to interact with the opposite sex in the way that they interact with one another. I have eight kids. The three oldest are boys. The five youngest are girls. When we are out somewhere, I expect my boys to run ahead and open the door for their sisters. If the sisters are carrying something the boys are expected to help their sisters. And I expect their sisters to be thankful for their brothers serving them in that way. You have to issue both directions.

But that has everything to do with the way they think about the world in terms of male and female and ultimately the way they are going to think about the issue of sexuality in the context of marriage.

3. UNAPOLOGETICALLY CHAMPION MARRIAGE AND CHILDREN.

Why are we so reluctant to talk to our children about sex? The primary reason is because we don't know what to say. One of the most controversial things I say in the context of my church and in other places that I have the opportunity to speak is that I tell my kids, "I don't care if you go to college. I want you to love Jesus and serve him and work hard. And I want you to get married." Now, a lot of evangelical parents are saying, "Listen, you don't want to get married at a young age because you need to go to college. You need to earn a living. You want to have these things. You want to be successful. You don't want to have kids too early." This way of thinking does not answer the question: what are they to think about these sexual urges that they have that God has given them? If you are telling them "just say no until marriage" but to not get married until they are thirty-three, that's a problem. Not many of them are going to wait. We must not say "just say no" to sexual activity outside of marriage—we must champion marriage. We must pray for them in relation with the expectation that they are going to get married.

When I go see babies born in the hospital one of the things

I do is I hold them and pray for them. I pray for their salvation. If it's a girl, I pray for God to provide her a husband one day that loves Christ. If it's a boy, I pray for God to provide a wife one day that loves Jesus and wants to serve him. I get the strangest looks. Not too long ago, I was in a hospital room like that, and the grandparents were very conservative theologically. I prayed for God to provide this little girl with a husband one day. I looked up and her granddad was glaring at me and said, "Why did you do that?" I asked him what he meant. He said, "What are you bringing up a husband for? You don't even know if she's going to get married. You don't know what she's going to be." Do you see that? He is trying to define her life at that moment, about what she might be, and marriage isn't in his thoughts. That's a problem if we are going to teach our children a proper view of sexuality.

4. UNHESITATINGLY ANSWER QUESTIONS WHEN ASKED.

Don't act intimidated when your children ask you questions related to sexuality. When you do that, the world has plenty of answers about issues related to sexuality. When we act intimidated, we act like sexuality is something to which Christianity doesn't speak directly. Answer the questions when you are asked. One approach that you might take though is to clarify the question, because you want to answer the question with truth, but you don't want to over-answer the question at a given age. You see the distinction there? For example, if they want to know why dad is different than mom, you don't want to over-answer that, but you want to satisfy it with truth. Oftentimes, I will say, "Does that answer your question?" And they will say yes, and you move on.

5. COMMIT TO READ THE BIBLE TOGETHER AS A FAMILY.

This year we started a plan to read the Bible together as families in our church. I told my staff that one of the reasons we are doing this is that it forces families to talk about things they don't normally talk about. I told them that we will start getting phone calls with people saying, "What do we do when we get to the sex parts? Do we just skip them?" No, you thank God that you have an opportunity to satisfy these questions and to lead your family.

6. BE THE FIRST PERSON TO TEACH YOUR CHILD ABOUT SEXUAL INTERCOURSE.

If sex is what you are, sexual intercourse—the conjugal act of marriage—is something you do. You want to shape how they think about this before they start hearing other things related to this. One of the things we do in our family is a manhood and womanhood retreat when our kids start getting to that age where you know that the questions are coming, they are unavoidable. I have used Dennis Rainey's *Passport to Purity* with my three sons. Rainey explains things that you can build on in a way that is helpful to you. One of the things that we do is to go do something fun. We are going to go to a series of ballgames or whatever, and I will ask, "Do you know what sex is?" You've been teaching them about sex in relation to their gender identity. You have been teaching them what it means to go from boyhood to manhood, from girlhood to womanhood, and this is saying: Okay, sexual intercourse is a part of that—let's talk about it. You want them to turn to you. You tell them, "I will be here for you."

7. USE DIRECT LANGUAGE, BUT AVOID BEING CRUDE OR MEDICAL.

Song of Solomon is a wonderful example in relation to this. Is Song of Solomon about Christ and the church or about a husband and a wife? The answer is yes. Marriage exists to point to the reality of Christ and the church. There is no conversation of marriage that isn't ultimately about the relationship between Christ and the church. It is unavoidable that certain things are addressed. But it's not crude. It's also not medical. You want to restrain your language. What I tell my sons and my wife tells our daughters is this: The medical term for that is this; you might hear this in the locker room; but this is the term we are going to use. We want to regain that language. Keep a sense of the mystery of the gospel as you talk about sex.

8. REACT TO SEXUAL SIN WITH THE GOSPEL AND NOT LIKE A PHARISEE OR SADDUCEE.

You want to raise a Pharisee? Have your child sin—let's say

in this instance it's sexual sin—and say, "I cannot believe you would do that!" If you are a believer, why wouldn't you believe that? If you want to raise a Sadducee then you say: You don't want to mess up your life. You have so much going for you and a bright future. You don't want to get anybody pregnant. Or you don't want to be pregnant. In other words, the status quo—let's live the good life. What you say to sexual sin is this: I am not surprised at all that you would do that. This is a struggle you will be in for the rest of your life, but I want you to understand that the issue is not just about messing up your life in terms of your goals. That's irrelevant. The issue is the gospel of Jesus Christ. The reason you ought to wait or the reason you ought not to do that is because this is all about the gospel. This is all about what it means to have a cruciform view of the world. And if you grasp after satisfaction outside of the plan and purposes of God, it will be empty. But if you struggle to obey God and believe the gospel of Jesus Christ—if your child is an unbeliever and you are dealing with sexual sin, you say: That's why you need Christ. There is forgiveness for these sins. We don't respond as Pharisees or Sadducees, but as Christians.

Your child will learn about sex. Your child will be taught how to respond to sexual urges. The only question is who will teach them. Pastors, will you challenge the parents in your church to give a faithful gospel education, which includes sex education? Satan would love for your children to be morally pure as long as that's not the fruit of the gospel, as long as it is abstract morality. With Satan, any path to self-righteousness, any path to self-exaltation is a good one. Satan doesn't hate morality. He hates the cross. May it be clear to our children that we want them to have a cross-centered understanding of their sexuality. We want them to have a cross-centered understanding of their body, because what we want for them more than anything is that they would determine to know nothing among anyone but Christ.

REVIEW QUESTIONS

1. *What should be our motive in seeking to obey God's commands regarding sexuality? How should we seek to instill this motive in our children?*

2. *What barriers and difficulties do you encounter when trying to teach your children about sexuality? How can you overcome those barriers?*

3. *How can you help your children understand the link between marriage and sex?*

═ 6 ═
THE TALK:
HOW TO DISCUSS SEXUALITY WITH TEENS IN YOUR HOME AND CHURCH

JIMMY SCROGGINS

Let me be honest from the beginning: I was much more confident about this topic until I actually had teenagers.

Teenagers will humble you, confound you, bother you, and keep you up at night. I remember all of the thoughts I had about parents who were struggling with their teenagers, feeling sorry for them, and thinking that if they could just get it together a little bit, they wouldn't have all these problems. When you have teenagers, you realize *you* need to get it together a little bit because *you* have problems. Without being too transparent and embarrassing everyone in my family, I will tell you that my eighteen-year-old, sixteen-year-old, fourteen-year-old, and twelve-year-old boys are one hundred percent red-blooded, viral, strapping young studs. These guys will do anything, and they have done anything. I have been involved with fistfights, the police department, deacons and their daughters, and the computer. I would love to tell you that all of my parenting philosophies and ways of talking to them about sex has resulted in a pain-free environment in our home, but that would be a complete lie.

I want to discuss the culture and affirm some things you already know. If you did not know these things about the culture, this is going to be very informative for you. I plan to gloss over a few things that you already know, that others have already said and written, and that are, in my opinion, pretty well established. Then I want discuss what churches can do to help families talk about sexuality. Some of these things will overlap with what parents can do. I may present myself as dogmatic and confident, but I want to assure you, as a pastor and as a father, I am very humble on this matter.

I was a teenager in the 1980s. Those were great decades because Bon Jovi was on the radio and we just had a great time. If you were a teenager in the 1980s, you know those were great years. Those were some of the last years that teenagers got to grow up without the Internet. Even though we had our own set of temptations and challenges, we did not have cell phones. Frankly, I think that made us safer. When I got together with my friends on Friday at school, we would make plans to all go to the movies: meet at a McDonald's parking lot (it was a small town, and that's where you went to meet or to fight), load up in cars however we could configure it, drive to another town where they actually had a movie theater, and watch movies. When evening rolled around, you would have to get in your car and make it to McDonald's by seven o'clock when you said, or for all you knew, everybody might have already left and you would be the only one there. If you didn't show up, nobody could find you. You were just out. That's the way we communicated. You would not talk to anybody from your school from three o'clock when you left until seven o'clock. There was no way to connect with them and no way to change plans.

I watch my kids. I actually have software on their phones, and I know how many times they text. My sixteen-year-old has texted the same girl 216 times since Monday, and she's texted him 432 times—women have twice as many words as men. These kids are in constant communication. They keep their stories straight. They change plans on the dime. They have meet-ups, tweet, etc. It's amazing what they can do.

Regarding entertainment choices, when I wanted to listen to music, even if my parents approved it or didn't approve it, I had to either turn on the radio or have in my possession a little silver disc called a CD or a cassette tape. We played them in our cars and in our room. I remember when my parents found my little brother listening to my contraband cassette tape that had rap music on it that was not following God's design. I got in some trouble. Parents could find your music and listen to it and see what was on it. Now it's all gone with the touch of a button.

When I was in high school and middle school, a lot of boys looked at pornography, but they ended up looking at the same pornography over and over because they only had a couple of magazines stashed somewhere. If anybody had a video, that was really dangerous stuff. If you got caught with that, you were in big trouble. Back then, somebody had to actually have the stuff in his hands. Today, it's a whole different world.

We live in an entirely different cultural situation for parents trying to raise kids. It is impossible to manage all of the technology to which children are exposed and using. We have as many filters and software as we can at our house. I've got software on their phones, and I do the best I can, but I am under no illusions that I am managing all of their technology. There is just no way. Everywhere they go there's Wi-Fi. They know that I have software on their phones, so they can use their friends' phones for anything that I don't want them to be able to do. I had to buy my boys tablets because it's required by their school. You are bound by this technology that frees them up to find things out, and you are not the gatekeeper for information. This really does change the game.

Because of all that, here's what we have: tremendous ambiguity in our culture. We have tremendous moral ambiguity among teenagers, even in our churches. I preached some messages on sexuality and family structure last fall, and one of the messages I did taught directly about gay marriage because it was in the news and there was an election coming up. Our church is very, very diverse.

It's racially diverse. It's ethnically diverse. It's linguistically diverse. It's sexual preference diverse. Hundreds of people come into our church that live together and are not married. They live together as husband and wife. We have other people who live together as wife and wife and husband and husband. We have these people attending our church all the time, and so when we talk about these things, we are not talking about people "out there." We are talking about people "in here." I try to be very clear and very sensitive when we talk about sexuality and family structure. I planned out my message to be as clear and sensitive as I could. In my opinion, it was a sensitivity masterpiece. I got a stool. I pulled the stool up to the edge of the stage and said, "Now guys, I want to have a little family conversation." I talked about how I believe that genetics plays a part, environment plays a part, culture plays a part, and our own sinful choices play a part. I said that we need to treat people kindly and that we are not going to do redneck theology. You will never hear an Adam and Steve joke from this platform. We just don't do that. That's not the way. It was probably the most sensitive and compassionate message ever delivered in evangelical history. Do you know what the buzz was in the teenage small groups right after that? The pastor's a bigot. Can you believe he preached that hate-filled diatribe against homosexuals? Don't you know that a lot of our friends are gay? Don't you know there are gay people that go to this church? Don't you know some of the parents of our youth group are gay? I honestly do not believe that there is a way to soften it more than I did. If I gave any more ground, I would have given it all up. Yet, the teenagers were very aware that at the end of all that compassion, I said that God's design is one man and one woman for life. These teenagers were saying, "Can you believe our pastor would preach a message that is so hateful?" That is the environment. It's morally ambiguous.

We are a very conservative church. We are inerrantists. We believe in inspiration. Most of the kids in our youth group go to Christian school or are homeschooled. If anybody should be onboard with what we are teaching about God's design, these kids should be onboard. But they are not. They are morally ambiguous.

After ambiguity, the culture is full of access. Technology gives kids unprecedented access. You cannot shut off the access—not just access to pornography, but access to information, access to ideas. They can Google "What does the Bible say about homosexuality?" and come up with all of the very best arguments by theologians and preachers who think that homosexuality and Christianity are compatible. With a few keystrokes, they can find recognizable—and in their minds, credible—preachers and theologians who will agree with the point of view that they already sort of embrace ignorantly, but willingly. Part of this moral ambiguity and access is not just to porn and sex information, but to points of view that are at variance with what Scripture teaches.

Next, there's radical autonomy in our society—this idea that the choices you make only affect you and don't affect anybody else. Which is a total lie, isn't it? There are no choices you can make that only affect you. Those choices do not exist. Every choice affects somebody else. Every single choice affects somebody else. Sin splatters. The sins of the father splatter to the third and fourth generation. So do the sins of the mother. So do the sins of the children. They just splatter. In my own family, when one of my sons falls into sin and gets into a mess and it starts to become difficult, do you not think that that affects my marriage? Of course it does. Does it not affect his brothers and his sisters? Yes, it will change the whole family dynamic. There are no decisions that only affect us.

This idea of ambiguity, matched with access and radical autonomy, creates an environment that is very volatile and very dangerous. And frankly, it's very difficult to master. In short, I am telling you some difficult news.

What does this mean for the teenagers that we are preaching to and teaching in our churches? First of all, it means that porn is a given. What do you think the chances are that my sons are going to graduate from high school having never once in their lives viewed pornography? It's not zero, but it's close. Some people my age and older like to think that it won't happen because he or she went all the way through high school without having ever looked at pornography—which I did not go through high school without ever looking at pornography. But for my sons, I think the chances are zero. Because of technology and access, it is a given that every teenager in your church has viewed and probably is viewing pornography—even the girls, although I think the girls view pornography differently. You say, "No, we've got some really sold-out teenagers in our church that would never do that." I hope and believe that you do, and I am sure that I do in my church as well. However, almost one hundred percent of your teenagers will, and that needs to inform the way that you talk to parents and the way that you talk to kids.

Secondly, sex is expected. In the early nineties, Josh McDowell had a pretty strong study, and some other groups have done it since then, that found that ninety percent of American teenagers lose their virginity before they graduate from high school. I don't think that statistic has gotten better. When the kids tell you that everybody at their school is having sex, they are very close to accurate. Only about sixty percent of evangelical kids have had sex before they graduate from high school. Sixty percent still is horrible, but it's a whole lot better than ninety percent. It means we are doing something. Something good is happening. Ninety to sixty is a significant difference, but you need to understand that sex is expected of them. As such, if they are not sexually active in their school, in their neighborhood, even in their Christian school, they are going to be countercultural. I am not talking about the culture at chapel in the Christian school or the culture on Thursday night at youth camp. I am talking about the culture every day, every week, every Friday, every Saturday. You know as well as I do that there is a veneer at the Christian school, and then there is what's really going on.

Finally, gay is okay. That is the environment. That is the ethos. That is the idea. Porn is a given. Sex is expected. Gay is okay.

There's one more idea that most teenagers can't articulate, but it's invading their minds: marriage is seen as a capstone, not a cornerstone. At some point after they get their education, start their career, buy a house, and travel the world, to cap it all off, they might get married. Then maybe to even cap it off a little bit more, have a baby. Most parents and churches actually think about it the same way, and they don't want to admit it. Ask your parents, what age do you think those kids ought to be getting married?

Do you know what God's design is? God's design is that, for almost everybody, marriage becomes a cornerstone upon which you build your life. It's not a capstone that completes your life. Children are not a capstone after a husband and wife get to know each other for years, make a lot of money, and then maybe have a baby. What did God say to Adam and Eve the very first day they were made? *The very first day.* Start being fruitful. Start multiplying. Give it a shot. He didn't say after you get the garden organized, build a bridge over there—no. Be fruitful and multiply. It's part of God's design. People in our society think that if you have kids, it's going to make it harder to be married. I believe that if you have kids, it makes it easier to be married in a lot of ways. It gives you something to hold you together.

We see moral ambiguity, access, and autonomy all flowing from the culture, but there are exceptions, although few and far between. There are children and families that are able to fight this, and able to teach their kids differently. When you speak to a group of teenagers and families in your church, this is where most of the kids are, and frankly, it's where a lot of the parents are. Let's say some of us do not live in an urban area—let's say some of us live in the Shire. If you live in the Shire—be thankful to live there. I am glad that there are parts of our country that are still the Shire, but what happens in the Shire? The hobbits sit there with their round doors and have their feasts and shoot off their fireworks, and they don't realize that the hordes from Mordor are advancing across the badlands, and there are guys like Aragorn out there fighting and trying to hold the line. Yet these guys in the Shire don't understand that it's coming. If you happen to live in the Shire, take great joy in that. We need some of you guys to do a great job of raising kids in the Shire. But if you live in an urban environment or if your church happens to have a lot of younger people in it, even in the Shire, what I've described here is probably resonating with you.

What are we going to do? First of all, to combat this situation in your church and your home, you have to build and rebuild a marriage culture. It's not rocket science: build and rebuild. Why do we have to rebuild? We've already built it. Every time a new person joins your church you have to start rebuilding again. Every time you reach somebody for Christ, every time a kid goes away to college and comes back, you have to build it and rebuild it, build it and rebuild it. You can never say you have built a marriage culture in your church. You have to rebuild it all the time because your church is turning over every three or four years in most places. Just about the time you're sick of talking about marriage, it's time to talk about it again. This is the key to the whole conversation that's going on in our society about marriage and family structure.

We talk about God's design as a marriage culture—we teach one man and one woman for life. We teach that children are a blessing and not a burden. We teach "naked and not ashamed." We hold a high view and a positive view of sexuality. We teach them these things over and over in different venues and different appropriate contexts for kids, teenagers, and adults.

As we do, we are going to get some pushback. One of the reasons evangelicals can't reach millennials very effectively is that most millennials are not married. The millennial generation started in 1981 according to demographers, making the oldest millennial thirty-three years old. What is the average age for first marriage for men in America right now? Twenty-eight. So most millennials are not married. When you start talking about marriage culture—husbands, love your wives; wives, love your kids; and kids are a blessing, not a burden—most of them are checking out. They're not married, and they are not thinking about getting married. For them, marriage is a capstone, not a cornerstone.

Boomers and Generation Xers also push back. Fifty percent of them are divorced and single, have been divorced, or have been married multiple times. The majority of the millennials are not married yet, and not sure they are going to get married yet. When you start doing marriage culture you have a bunch of people going, "Hey, what about us?"

We have to establish and reestablish and build and rebuild a marriage culture. You have to teach to it. You have to program to it. You have to honor it. You have to promote it and recognize that you are going to get some pushback. Of course, we want to be accommodating, compassionate, and encouraging to people who are rebuilding marriages, who are getting married again, who are single, who are single moms or single dads. Yet, we must build and rebuild a marriage culture. In my opinion, we cannot apologize for that. We cannot back off. We have got to be hammered down on building a marriage culture so when millennials ask, "What about me?" you say, "I'm talking about you. You need to get married. You need to rearrange your priorities." They'll respond, "It's better not to get married than to marry the wrong person." Yeah, no joke. But marry the right person. It's not as complicated as some make it out to be. We want to make sure we are building and rebuilding this marriage culture, and we are talking about it all the time.

Here are some ideas to consider for parents and for pastors. First of all, if you are going to talk about sexuality, you can't talk about sexuality without talking about marriage. You should never in any context have a conversation about sexuality without talking about marriage—not to preschoolers, not to children, not from the pulpit, not to tweens, not to teenagers. You should always, in an age-appropriate manner, talk about marriage every time you talk about sex because there is no design for sex outside of marriage as far as God is concerned. There is no gospel representation for sex outside of marriage. If you've got staff members, train them. Don't let your children's people talk about it unless you are talking about marriage. Train your youth leaders to talk about it and then talk about marriage. Do you know who the Church Lady is from Saturday Night Live? Never, ever let that woman talk about sex in your church. You have got to be careful how you talk about it and who talks about it.

Have these talks early, not late. The very best time to teach God's design to parents is in pre-marriage counseling. That is the time in our culture when you are going to have the most effective traction talking about God's design for sexuality. At our church, the majority of people who sign up for pre-marriage class are living together and not married. When I start teaching this to them, most of the time they are shocked, absolutely flabbergasted. They'll ask, "Are you telling me that I am not supposed to be having sex with her at all?" We tell them, "Yes, is it is God's design for you to have sex only in the context and the covenant of committed marriage." So they ask, "What am I going to do?"

Before I went to southern Florida, I had all these little rules that I would outline—like if you are going to get married and you are living together, you've got to move out for six months. If you have those at your church, more power to you. After living in southern Florida for about six months, I realized there are too many. I don't have the manpower and energy to keep up with all these people. Their lives and their morals and their relationships are so sordid and twisted, I can't untie the pretzel for all these people. Some people get to pastor like James in the city of Jerusalem and have people with an orderly sort of society in a cultural context that at least somewhat points towards God's design, even though not everybody's a Christian. Some of us are like Paul in Corinth, and man, these people are sleeping with the temple prostitutes and there's incest and more. When you go there, you can't go unwrap the pretzel for all these people. It's too messed up.

I tell people in this type of situation: if you are a believer in Jesus now, let's start trying to pursue God's design from right here. Like the old song says, why don't we "love the one you're with," from now on? We started doing that, and we started doing weddings everywhere. I've done weddings in living rooms, out by the beach, in the backyard, and on the side of the church. I did a wedding last year for two in this situation who didn't want to move out and had kids. I said, "Let's just get married Saturday." So, they went and got their certificate, came to the church, and there wasn't anybody there but them and me. I didn't even ask the facilities people. I just unlocked the door and went in. They brought their computers, set them up on chairs, and Skyped with all their family members from Ohio and New Jersey. That's the only Skype wedding I've ever done.

I saw a couple yesterday that I married out by the Intracoastal Waterway. They've been together for a year and a half, and she's expecting. They brought their friends to church for the first time yesterday. Their friends are living together and not married, and they have a baby. We are going to work with them. We are doing weddings all the time. We decided we are going to help people get married, and help them get there because this is part of establishing a marriage culture.

If you go to parents of fifteen-, sixteen-, seventeen-year-olds and start to teach them that dating is a bad idea—too late, Jack! These people are hanging on for dear life now. They are trying to get their kids to college without killing someone in a vehicle or getting somebody pregnant. That's all they're trying to do. It's too late. Forget trying to educate parents of seventeen-year-olds about how everything that they have done so far is not exactly right. You would be much better off starting with parents of preschoolers and in your pre-marriage class. It's the best place to teach God's design and to teach a marriage culture—early, not late.

Give tools to your parents to help them talk to their kids about sex and do it early, not late; younger, not older. There's not *the* talk. There's a conversation. And the conversation starts when they are little kids. Start by affirming the gender that God has assigned to them and affirming some of the roles that they are going to play as a result of that gender. You can say to an eighteen-month-old little girl, "You look just as pretty as Mommy; one day you will probably be a mommy. One day you will probably get married." You can say to your sons, "Help me take out the trash because you have got to learn to work. One day you are going to be husband and a dad, and you have to help provide for your family." It's going to be very important. It's a conversation that you are going to have all the time, and then there will be a time when you have the talk. You will put the cards on the table and say, "God gave you this and gave them one of those." They'll think it's gross and weird.

I remember the first time I ever I told my son. I made the decision because of the questions he was asking and because of some things that were in the news. It was my oldest, James, and I just told him everything. I mean everything. He sat there quietly for a few minutes. We were riding in the car, driving through the mountains. He said, "So you are telling me that every time you and Mom have had a baby you had to do that first?"

I said, "We had to."

He was quiet for a few more minutes and finally said, "Well, I can promise you one thing, Dad. I am probably going to get married one day, but I am never ever going to do that."

I said, "We'll see." He's changed his mind now. He's eighteen. He's very interested.

You have got to talk early, not late. Sexual information is pursuing the kids in your home and in your church. It is in the air. It's in the atmosphere. It's over the airwaves. Sexual information is pursuing them like the hounds of hell. You need to get there first and a little bit early. If it's a little bit too heavy, believe me, they will grow into it faster than you think.

Secondly: more, not less. Give them more information than they need as opposed to less information than they need. Somebody will give them more information than you want them to get.

Dennis Rainey says: Who is better equipped to talk to my ten-year-old about sex, me or the other ten-year-old morons running around the neighborhood? Me. I know a lot more about sex. I have had sex thousands of times. I know exactly what I'm talking about. I have read about it. I have studied it. I've worked at it. I know a lot about this subject way more than any kid in elementary school, way more than any kid in middle school, way more than any kid in high school, way more than any kid in college. I know more about this than any kid in college in America because they are just not old enough. I've been at this twenty years. I have made it a very important part of my life. You have got to be the one that gives them the information. You have got to do it age appropriately. Marriage and sex is all over the Bible. Every Bible story has sex in it. Every Bible story has family. Every Bible story has marriage in it. Talk about it as often as the Bible does and as clearly as the Bible does.

Thirdly: be clear, not crude. It is in vogue to be crude from the pulpit or the platform when talking about sex. That is a horrible mistake. Just because the culture has dragged it down into the gutter and made it a dirty thing, don't affirm the culture's view of sex as dirty by getting down in the gutter with them to talk about it. It is not necessary. Sex is mysterious. It's fun to talk about. It's kind of funny. It's a little embarrassing. That's really the way that God designed it, because there is a mystery to it. Let the mystery speak for itself. Let the fun speak for itself. You don't have to be crude. Be clear when you talk about sex; don't be crude. We should be as direct and clear as the culture, but we should not be crude. Crude speech and crude talking, Paul says, are anti-gospel. Don't get down in the gutter, thinking we're connecting because we got just as dirty as they did on whatever show. We didn't connect, or we connected in the wrong way. If you believe the gospel, we should be holding up a view of sex that is purer and higher and more fun and more reverent and more mysterious than anyone else. Don't get crude, and don't allow your youth pastor to get crude. Don't allow your college pastor to get crude. For Pete's sake—fire your children's pastor if he gets crude!

Talk about design. Don't talk about "don't." Design is better than "don't." If you ask most teenagers what they learned in youth group, they will tell you two things: I am supposed to love Jesus and not have sex. If that is really what they are getting out of our youth program, we need to do something different. There has got to be more to this than: I want to love Jesus and I want to not have sex. Not having sex is a horrible goal. I don't think it's biblical. I don't think it's gospel. Our goal is not for our kids to not have sex. Our goal is for our kids, yes, to love Jesus, but to embrace the gospel and to live out God's design in every aspect of their lives, including their sexuality. Talk about God's design; it's a great phrase. God has designed it this way, and we need to help them think about it.

Be positive, not negative. That's why I say don't let the Church Lady talk. If we can't talk about sex in a positive, exciting way to where people want to do more of it, then we are talking about it wrong. Christians ought to want to have sex more and more joyfully and more creatively than anybody else as a result of our preaching and teaching and our understanding of the gospel. You know that song "Why Should the Devil Have All the Good Music?" Why should the devil have all the good sex? Our God created it. He designed it. It was part of us before there was the fall. So, talk about God's design. Don't just talk about what not to do. Be positive not negative.

Encourage, do not condemn. We are in the situation I described where sex is expected and porn is the norm with our kids. Generation Xers are raising our teenagers right now. Most Generation Xers have had multiple sexual partners in their lifetime. The current generation is being raised by a previous generation that really was morally ambiguous and autonomous, with certain amount of access. We're dealing with multigenerational sexual sin. It's no wonder nobody wants to draw lines. No one can say, "I did it this way." Almost everybody is going to have to say, "I didn't do it that way, but it would be nice if you did; if you don't, here's a condom." We have to recognize that. We have got to encourage people not to condemn people. When parents come to our church, they should not feel condemned and marginalized. They should feel encouraged in this area. We ought to be the Home Depot of teenagers and children and sexuality. You guys can do it, and we can help. That ought to be our motto. Parents can do it, and church can help.

David Prince may get in a fistfight with me about this, but I think it's better to talk about sexuality with young people in terms of management as opposed to triumphalism. It's not helpful to talk to people about being delivered from sexual temptation because I don't know that it's really possible until the eschaton. We ought to be talking, especially to our young people and our teenagers, about managing their sexuality. Their sexuality is a good thing that God has given them. How can we help them manage it for their own good and for God's glory? How can we help them manage it towards the maximization of their joy, the glory of God and the magnification of the gospel? For the sake of an example, let's take masturbation. Almost one hundred percent of boys are going to do this at some point in their life. Telling boys there is some silver bullet of verses to memorize to make it not an issue for them, for the rest of their life, until they get married, makes you kind of like a liar. I am not saying, everybody have at it. But I am saying we need to talk to them about managing their sexuality in a way that makes sense and in a way that can actually help them think gospel thoughts and about God's design in a helpful way. If we act like there is something they should be able to do to resist all these urges and impulses, what happens when they fail—as they all do? They doubt their salvation because of the way we taught it. They think, "If I was really a Christian, then I wouldn't be doing this." And I hate to break it to you—you don't need a testimony here—but if that made people lose their salvation, all of you would go to hell. We've got to talk about managing desires and drives that are good, but managing them in a way that maximizes God's glory and our joy and magnifies the gospel. That is part of building a marriage culture.

Lastly, no matter how you teach it or talk about it, because our culture is so fallen and twisted in this area, you have got to saturate this whole thing with the grace of God. You have got to be talking about the gospel of Jesus and the grace of God, and it's got to saturate our teaching on sexuality. Here's a model that we use in talking about sexuality. This is a model that we use to talk about a lot of different things, but we've developed this model out of our pre-marriage classes with our sexually immoral pre-marriage people. We teach that God has a design for sexuality and family structure. Of course, it explains that pretty clearly in the first two chapters of Genesis. But what happens if we depart, individually and as a society, from God's design? Any time we depart from God's design, it is sin. When we depart from God's design, inevitably we end up in brokenness. That is why we feel cheap and empty and used and guilty. That's why we have abortions, why we have divorces, and why we are all messed up. We're all warped, addicted to pornography, and in these chat rooms on the Internet, because we ended up in brokenness. We are always going to try to find some way to escape or alleviate the brokenness that we are feeling, but none of it is going to work. It's just going to take us deeper and deeper into more and more brokenness. There's really only one thing that we can do. This brokenness feels like a bad thing when you are experiencing it, but it's not a bad thing. It's actually a good thing because the Bible says that the kindness of God is actually leading us to a certain place. It's called repentance.

"Repent" means to change your mind and change your direction. God wants us to repent of our sins, change our mind about the direction we have been going, recognize our departure from his design, and believe the good news about God's grace—the gospel.

The gospel is what we need to turn towards and what we need to remind ourselves of, that Jesus died on the cross for our sins and took our shame and our guilt on himself. We don't need to bear that anymore. We don't have to carry it around like a big weight. We can let Jesus have all that. We can receive the righteousness of Jesus, and we have repented of our sins. We believe.

After we embrace the gospel, we can begin to recover and pursue God's design from wherever we are right now. Maybe your daughter had sex before marriage. She departed from God's design, and now she feels cheap and empty and used. Her boyfriend dumped her and she almost tried to cut and kill herself. She was experiencing brokenness, but that brokenness that feels like a bad thing is kind of a good thing because it's God getting your daughter's attention. God wants her to change her mind and to repent of her sins and to believe in the gospel of Jesus. If she will do that, God can clean her up on the inside and make her totally clean. Jesus can take her shame upon himself, and she can have the righteousness of Jesus. Can she go back and become a virgin all over again? No. She had those experiences. Can she erase her memories? No. But from right here, right now—she can begin to recover and pursue God's design from right here and right now because of the gospel.

This doesn't work for people who aren't Christians. It works for Christians. This is how the Christian life works, isn't it? So, if you find yourself looking at pornography, what do you do? Do you go jump in the river? No. You might be experiencing brokenness because you looked at pornography. Repent and remind yourself of the gospel of Jesus. You now have resurrection power to live wisely and to overcome these things. Do you act from now on like you've never looked at pornography? No. But you can begin to recover and begin to pursue God's design from right here where you are.

Take any issue you want and this will help you talk about it in a way that's encouraging instead of condemning. We've found that it helps people and helps us talk to them in a way that makes sense and doesn't feel like we are judging them. And they are exposed to the truth of the gospel.

REVIEW QUESTIONS

1. *What are you doing to protect your children against pornography? Are there additional steps that you could take?*

2. *What unbiblical messages are your children hearing about sexuality? What can you do as a parent to counter those lies with God's truth?*

3. *How should Christian parents respond when their children fall into sexual sin? How should this response be shaped by the gospel?*

4. What does it mean to cultivate a "marriage culture" in our churches?

═ 7 ═
FINALLY FREE:
THE GOSPEL AND
PORNOGRAPHY

HEATH LAMBERT

Proverbs 7

I want to tell you a story about my mother. It was late January 2010, and she hadn't been feeling well since Christmastime. No big deal. She was feeling a little more tired than usual and wasn't quite herself. As she increasingly lost her appetite and became even more fatigued, our family decided that she needed to go to the doctor for a checkup. The doctor knew there was something wrong but couldn't figure out what it was. We sent her for more tests and more tests after that. After several weeks she was diagnosed with terminal cancer. As the doctor sat with her in the hospital, he explained that there was a zero percent cure rate for cancer at this stage, and unfortunately, she had only a matter of weeks to live. And he was correct. After a few short weeks, I was standing in a funeral home with my mother's casket. It was a shock. You don't plan for something like that.

I tell you this because I think that the church is confronting a similar reality across our congregations. The church is filled with people in the pews who look as if everything is okay. Everything seems fine—maybe not quite what we would expect, but basically everything is okay. And yet there is this silent killer of pornography all across our churches. Pornography represents the greatest moral crisis in the history of the church. There are all sorts of moral problems that we are confronting. But porn is something that evangelicals can do in a dark room, behind a closed door, after they have railed against homosexual marriage and talked about conservative theology. The greatest threat to the church today is not the culture's embrace of homosexual marriage. That is a problem, and I'm thankful we are talking about it, but I think a greater threat to the church today is the Christian pastor, the Christian schoolteacher, the Christian Bible college and seminary student who exalts sound theology, who points to the Bible, and then retreats to a basement computer to indulge in an hour or two or three of Internet pornography. And it is in that crisis that I want to draw attention to Proverbs 7.

I want to take this passage in two large chunks: what it says about pornography, and then what it says to leaders about pornography. When this was written, people didn't have pornography in the way that we have it today. But make no mistake, Proverbs

7 is about pornography. The "forbidden woman" in Proverbs 7 is the woman of pornography—the pornographic harem that men and women of today are feasting their eyes on when they look at the Internet. Though this passage doesn't use the word pornography, it has implications for our modern experience of it.

Proverbs 7 highlights four things about pornography:

1. THE FORBIDDEN WOMAN OF PORNOGRAPHY MUST BE AVOIDED.

The young man in Proverbs 7 does not avoid the forbidden woman. Our churches are filled with young men and young women and husbands and pastors who are not avoiding the Proverbs 7 woman. This passage emphasizes that she must be avoided. In verse 7, the teacher says, "I have seen among the simple, I have perceived among the youths, a young man lacking sense, passing along the street near her corner, taking the road to her house in the twilight, in the evening, at the time of night and darkness." The young man is not where should be. He is taking the road to her house. He knows where he is. He knows the road to her house. He knows where he is, and he goes there anyway. The young man is at a place he shouldn't be and at a time he shouldn't be there. It is getting dark. There is no accountability in his life. He is all alone at a place he should not be.

This passage invites us to consider all the strategies that we need to implement in our lives to combat pornography. Romans

13:14 says, "Put on the Lord Jesus Christ and make no provision for the flesh to gratify its desires." Have you ever thought about how practical that passage is? It encourages us to consider all of the ways that we make provision for the flesh—in this case pornography. It invites us to consider all the times when we are where we should not be at a time we should not be there, and then it encourages us to get rid of those opportunities, to make no provision for them. We need to eliminate those temptations. How do we access tempting material? How are we making provision for the flesh? What do we do when we are alone? What are we doing to protect ourselves from being near this forbidden woman? It's a physical address in the ancient world. Today, in the context of pornography, it's an address that begins with www.

Matthew 5:29–30 says, "If your right eye causes you to sin, tear it out and throw it away. It is better that you lose one of your members than that your whole body be thrown into hell. If your right hand causes you to sin, cut it off and throw it away. It is better that you lose one of your members than that your whole body go into hell." I am aware of a lot of strategies to help eliminate the problem of pornography that overlook the practicalities of avoiding the temptation. There are some people who think that all we need to do is just believe this, that, or the other truth. But the Bible emphasizes practical strategies in eliminating temptations. This forbidden woman of pornography must be avoided. God wouldn't tell us this if it weren't good for us. God wouldn't tell us this if it were not so.

But you can't just avoid her. Behavior change is not enough. It's not enough to know where she is and just steer clear. And the reason that is not enough is because she has powerful seductive appeal.

2. THE FORBIDDEN WOMAN OF PORNOGRAPHY IS TEMPTING.

The Bible is very honest about this. Verse 5 says the wise father tells the son that he wants to keep him "from the forbidden woman, from the adulteress with her smooth words." Verse 21 talks about the seductive speech that she uses to persuade him. The forbidden woman of pornography is a tempting seductress. And these temptations sink down into your heart. Verse 25 implores, "Let not your heart turn aside to her ways." That's why it is about more than behavior. It's about a heart that is attracted to her seductions, and so we have to think about these temptations that woo us.

There are several temptations of the forbidden woman. As verse 15 reminds, one temptation is that it's about *you*: "So now I have come out to meet you, to seek you eagerly, and I have found you." The lie of the forbidden woman of pornography, the temptation, is that she is there for *you*. She wants to make *you* feel good, not your wife, not your girlfriend. *She* wants to make you feel good. She is there for you, and it is a temptation. It's a temptation, appealing to our most base desires for life to be all about us.

Another temptation is that it will be fun: "I have spread my couch with coverings, colored linens from Egyptian linen; I have perfumed my bed with myrrh, aloes, and cinnamon. Come, let us take our fill of love till morning; let us delight ourselves with love" (verses 16–18). She doesn't say it's going to be boring. She doesn't say it's going to hurt. She doesn't say it's going to ruin your life. The forbidden woman of pornography only holds up the pretty, forbidden fruit. She doesn't tell you that the first bite is going to kill you. It's going to be fun.

The temptation of the forbidden woman of pornography is that nobody will ever know. Look at verses 19–20, "For my husband is not at home; he has gone on a long journey; he took a bag of money with him; at full moon he will come home." We are safe. The coast is clear. The husband is gone; he's got a bag of money; he doesn't need anything; he is coming back at full moon—we can do whatever we want. The lie of pornography is that nobody will ever know. You wouldn't do it if you thought someone would find out. You wouldn't do it if you knew you were going to lose your ministry position. You wouldn't do it if you knew your wife was going to leave. You wouldn't do it if you knew your kids were going to think you were a pervert. The lie is: nobody has to know.

Here's another temptation of the forbidden woman—you don't have to worry. She says her husband is not at home. She's got a husband. She's got somebody taking care of her. No strings attached. One of the most awful realities about Christians looking at Internet pornography is that we consume these women without a care in the world for their salvation or the problems they are facing. These are women that need us to move toward them with the love and the care of Jesus Christ. We make their problems somebody else's problem. It's one of the temptations of this forbidden woman.

The forbidden woman of pornography must be avoided, but that's hard because the forbidden woman of pornography is a temptress. And so we have to pierce through the temptations with truth.

3. THE FORBIDDEN WOMAN OF PORNOGRAPHY IS A LIAR.

Those lies that pornography tells you, they're just that. They are not the truth. It's advertising. This is what verses 22 and 23 say: "All at once he follows her, as an ox goes to the slaughter, or as a stag is caught fast till an arrow pierces its liver; as a bird rushes into a snare; he does not know that it will cost him his life." The Bible is honest that the forbidden woman of pornography is a temptress. It sounds fun. But the Bible also tells you the truth that you won't hear from her: that you will die. It will end in destruction. All of the creatures in these verses walked willingly to their death because they don't know what they are doing. It's a warning to people who believe the lies of the forbidden woman.

Proverbs 7 combats the lies with the truth. We're asked to let the truths sink into our hearts in verses 2–3: "Keep my commandments and live." You don't have to die. You don't have to walk into the snare. You don't have to go to the slaughter. You don't have to be caught fast. The Bible combats the lie with truth.

I want to break a rule that I have with myself. One of my personal rules when I talk or write about pornography is that I don't underline the problem, because if you read about pornography for very long, you will find out that what people like to write about is how bad the problem is. They like to talk about how much money the porn industry makes. They like to talk about how many movies are made. They like to talk about the carnage that happens to actors in pornography and to consumers of pornography. And because I am committed to biblical counseling, the people that I am talking to already know it's wrong. I don't need to engage in a persuasive argument that it's wrong. I want to help people. Most of my ministry is about strategies to change and help.

Below are a few facts that I have picked at random to underline the tragedy that is this industry:

- *Nearly 100 percent of performers in the pornography industry have an STD.* You don't see that when you are watching the Internet. That's not in the advertisement.

- *Ninety percent of those in the industry are involved in some type of drug abuse.* It could be marijuana. It could be ecstasy. It could be alcohol. Some people have asked why so many people in the porn industry are on drugs. Here's what one performer says: Guys are punching you in the face. Your body is damaged and torn. You're viewed as an object, not as a human being with a spirit. People do drugs in porn because they can't deal with the way they are being treated. You don't see that between takes these women have to go get high. They have to go throw up because of what they are being asked to do so they can collect their paycheck when it's all over.

- *Twelve is now the average age for the first exposure of pornography to boys.* That is hardcore, moving pornography. In my ministry I encounter eighteen- to twenty-four-year-old men who cannot remember a time when they did not have unfettered access to pornography. If twelve is the average age, it means that some people are being exposed to it a lot earlier. Here's the reality: sociologists who write about this will tell you that we have no idea what kind of generation we are creating. We haven't tested it yet. We don't know what it's like to have a nation of grown men who were taught about sex from Internet pornography.

- *Fifty-six percent of divorce cases cite one of the partners as having some level of enslavement to pornography.*

That's the truth behind all the "fun" in verses 15 and 16. It will kill you. We have to fight the tempting lies of the forbidden woman in pornography with the truth of God's word. But that truth alone won't stop people from looking at pornography.

4. THE FORBIDDEN WOMAN OF PORNOGRAPHY CAN ONLY BE RESISTED BY THE GRACE OF JESUS CHRIST.

The forbidden woman of pornography can only be resisted by the grace of Jesus Christ. It's not enough to change your behavior so you can keep away from her. That will work for a little while; it won't change you. It's not enough to combat the lies with the truth. Ultimately it will make you feel guiltier when you look at it. The forbidden woman of pornography can only be resisted by the grace of Jesus Christ. "Say to wisdom, 'You are my sister,' and call insight your intimate friend, to keep you from the forbidden woman" (Prov. 7:4-5). What do you need to resist the forbidden woman? Wisdom.

Scripture says that Jesus Christ is our source of wisdom. In Colossians 2:2-3, Paul affirms this: "I write that your hearts may be encouraged, being knit together in love, to reach all the riches of full assurance of understanding and the knowledge of God's mystery, which is Christ, in whom are hidden all the treasures of wisdom and knowledge." All the treasures of wisdom and knowledge are hidden in Christ. Another passage is I Corinthians 1:30: "And because of him you are in Christ Jesus, who became to us wisdom from God, righteousness and sanctification and redemption." The wisdom that frees us from the shackles of the forbidden woman is a man named Jesus of Nazareth, and in him alone can you be free from the scourge that is pornography.

I am pleading with the church to have practical strategies. We need to have wisdom about how to gouge out our eye and cut off our hand. But those behaviors won't be enough if we are not teaching people to draw near to Jesus Christ. The first appeal when we are helping someone is to say, "Don't do that, get software on your computer, get an accountability partner." All of those things are great, but the first thing we need to say is to look to Jesus Christ, who is the personification of wisdom. He will set you free.

Proverbs 7 is for Christian leaders, for pastors, and for ministry heads. It exemplifies a man in spiritual authority. "My son, keep my words and treasure up my commandments with you" (Prov. 7:1). We see this man in spiritual authority teaching someone under his authority, if he would listen. He imparts wisdom to those who hear. He has some insight and some experience that he wants to share with this person who is listening to him: "At the window of my house I have looked out through my lattice, and I have seen among the simple, I have perceived among the youths a young man lacking sense" (Prov. 7:6).

Let me say a few things to Christian leaders about this. First, we have to embrace the wisdom that we see here. We have to talk about the forbidden woman of pornography in the same way that the author of Proverbs does. I've talked to pastors all across the country, who say one of two things: Pornography is not a problem in my church. Or, I can't talk about pornography from the pulpit. For those who say it's not a problem in their church: It is a problem in your church, you just don't know it. That's what's so deadly about it. You don't know it. For those who say they can't talk about it: Yes, you can. You have to. If your job is to preach the whole counsel of God, then you must talk about this. If we do not share this, if we overlook it, it's folly. It's foolishness.

We need to embrace the wisdom here as it exemplifies talking honestly about a hard topic. If we overlook it, it's folly. But here's the thing: if we teach it, but we don't observe it in our own lives, then we are hypocrites. And here's the dirty little secret: church leaders are struggling with this. If we teach it, but don't observe it, we are hypocrites. The Lord, who is the definition of purity, will not honor as holy the ministries of men who are hiding sin in the dark.

We need to talk about this. We need to appeal to people to be on guard about this—not just talk about it in some dispassionate way. "Keep my commandments, and live; Keep my teaching as the apple of your eye" (verse 2). I know what happens when you go down this road. "Let not your heart turn aside to her ways. Many a victim has she laid low, and all her slain are a mighty throng" (Prov. 7:25-27). Draw near to wisdom. Get close to Jesus. We have to appeal to our people to do this. The stakes are death.

Where do we go from here? What do we do? Here are three things.

1. AS CHRISTIAN LEADERS WE NEED TO PURSUE ACCOUNTABILITY.

Did you know that a recent statistic says 75 percent of pastors do not make themselves accountable to anyone for their activity on the Internet? In a world, culture, or church where we are dying because of this problem, that is not wise. Let's commit today that we will make ourselves accountable on this matter. Let's make ourselves accountable with our life and with our desires. All of us need to find somebody, another man if you are a guy, another woman if you are a woman, somebody in our life, and maybe two or three that know everything—who know the struggles, know the secret thoughts of our heart, and are able to pray for us and hold us accountable. We need to expose the darkness to the light and be accountable with our life and with our desires.

We also need to be accountable with the devices we use to access the Internet. I can't throw this out as a law—the Bible doesn't give me the freedom to do that—but I want to commend as strongly as I can that if you are in a Christian leadership position, you do something to have protection on your Internet. We need to pursue this kind of accountability in our own lives so that we are not hypocrites.

2. ADDRESS YOUR PEOPLE.

Maybe you are a pastor. Maybe you are a dad. Maybe you are a mom. Maybe you are a president. But address your people on this. Address your children. Talk to them about strategies they can use to protect themselves. I cannot imagine being a pastor of a church that has no wisdom for parents or grandparents about what you can do with your computers, iPhones, and tablets to be sure that your home is protected. We must have strategies. We need pastors who are growing up in wisdom about how to help people who struggle. There are pastors who come to me and say, "I have an eighteen-year-old in my church who is looking at pornography three hours a day, and I have no idea what to do." You know the Bible has answers for that. That's not some crazy, extreme situation that the Bible doesn't address. That's a normal life-and-godliness issue that the Bible has wisdom for, and faithfulness in Christian ministry today means faithfulness with those strategies. We need to address our people, whether they are our kids or our grandkids or the people in our church.

3. WE NEED TO AWAKEN THE WORLD TO THIS PROBLEM.

I wrote *Finally Free* because I wanted to provide strategies to people who didn't know how to help. I wanted to provide strategies to guys who were in a struggle they felt like they were losing. I'm glad this book has helped people, but the thing that concerns me is that it's not enough. The book is about picking up a mess, but it doesn't stop the problem. I am asking for, and praying for, evangelicals to get serious about awakening the world to this problem. Evangelicals have tenderly and tenaciously taken up many causes. I pray that together we can take up this cause and begin to say that enough is enough. No more will we sit back and allow this cultural decay. No longer will we sit back and allow this attack on our women and our churches and our homes. I am asking for and I am praying for a movement to fight for and protect women, families, and churches from this scourge that is destroying us.

And here is the reality: We are entering a world where we are the ones who understand just how tragic this is. I am praying for a concerted effort on the part of Christians and Christian leaders to protect our homes, our churches, and our children. We need to be the ones who take a courageous message of love to a culture that Jesus Christ came to set free from sin. By his grace, and by his grace alone, you can be set free from your sexual sin.

This is a big vision. It will take a lot of effort, but it will take effort that we are assured we will have grace for, and Jesus Christ is on the cause of righteousness. There is no grasp of porn so tight that the grace of Jesus can't break it. That's true in your life, and that's true in our culture. Together let's turn our eyes on Jesus Christ as we turn from this in our own lives and as we lead our churches towards greater purity.

REVIEW QUESTIONS

1. *How can we avoid the trap of pornography? How can you establish accountability in this area of your life?*

2. *What lies are associated with pornography? How does the gospel of Christ refute those lies?*

3. *What should we teach those whom God has placed in our care (especially*

our children) about resisting pornography and pursuing purity?

— 8 —
A BRIEF REFLECTION ON WOMEN AND SEXUALITY

TRILLIA NEWBELL

A few years ago a friend told me of a struggle, a deeply personal struggle. I had no reason to suspect that this friend struggled with much. We all struggle, but I had known her for so long and no major temptations had ever surfaced.

She was a committed church member, served faithfully on ministry teams, and basically had everything together on the outside. But she had a secret: at night she would watch pornography, and this wasn't a one-time occurrence. It had become a habit, even an addiction. I wasn't shocked by her confession. We are all sinners. I simply wondered how many other women were secretly struggling with pornography? I'll come back to her story.

I had another friend with a different situation. She did not struggle with sexual sin. On the contrary, she had a secret and a secret shame. She had been married for fifteen years and had never shared with anyone, including her husband, that she had been sexually assaulted. She was afraid to share, afraid because she feared she would be shamed. She wasn't raped, but she was assaulted, and remained fearful for many, many years.

Women face various temptations and difficulties while living in this fallen world. When it comes to sexuality, women are suffering and struggling. Most of the books and articles on this topic are for men. I will offer a few ways we can minister to women in this important area.

We must start by remembering that men and women are both created in the image of God. We are created equal, but we are created different, and this does indeed affect our sexuality. We were created before sin came into the world. The fall of man wreaked havoc on what was perfect in this world, specifically affecting women and our sexuality. We know in Genesis 3 that the punishment for Eve's disobedience was that women would have pain in childbearing, but we know it doesn't end there. Women are reminded every four to six weeks through our menstrual cycle of the death and destruction of the fall. Miscarriage, hormonal imbalance, and cancers attack our organs that produce life and give sustenance. We live with the unfortunate reality that because of the sin in this world, women are objectified. We objectify ourselves in magazines and by supporting sexually explicit images, and we are objectified by men. This is our reality. What was once pure and undefiled is now covered in shame and sin. Adam and Eve were naked in the garden and experienced no problem until they sinned. After sinning, they were ashamed of their nakedness. What was pure and should never have been an object of sinful lust had to then be covered. Understanding the fall and how it affects us is foundational to this conversation.

Here's my first point. Statistics can be skewed and inaccurate, but they often give us at least a small glimpse into a problem of which we may be unaware. Justin Holcomb records in his book *Rid of My Disgrace* that according to the Bureau of Justice, women sixteen to nineteen years old had the highest rate of sexual victimization of any age group. In my own research, I discovered the FBI named sexual assault as one of the most underreported crimes. Some stats show that one out of every six women in the United States has been raped or assaulted. Church pews, therefore, may be filled with women who have suffered under the hands of another person, and these women may be too embarrassed to say a word, like my friend that I told you about earlier. Women can carry embarrassment and shame, and carry it alone. Forget the numbers for a moment and simply picture your sisters' faces. These are the women that we want to care for, victims who need to be rid of their disgrace and find grace, love, and the healing power of the gospel. Leaders must be prepared to care for victims through Caesar and the church. If a victim approaches you, any crime must be reported to legal authorities, and proper church authority must be exercised.

In addition to sexual assault, another problem pastors cannot afford to ignore is sex trafficking. In October 2013 news outlets across the nation reported the rescue of more than one hundred teenage victims of sex trafficking. The youngest victim was thirteen years old. The FBI estimates that nearly 293,000 American youths currently are at risk of becoming victims of commercial sexual exploitation. Victims are often young, from broken families, or orphans. They are taken, sold, and forced into sex or prostitution. Most are girls, but boys are also exploited. Sex trafficking is a global issue. The FBI reports that it is the fastest growing business of organized crime and the third largest criminal enterprise in the world. Pastors and leaders must be aware of this problem. Don't assume that it can't happen in your area. The good news is that there are ministries available to help. The International Justice Mission, Sower of Seeds, and Project Red Light Rescue are just a few. The International Mission Board of the Southern Baptist Convention shares Christ and serves those in spiritual and physical need, through avenues such as OneLife's One Woman and One Brothel projects. Several resources are available at www.erlc.com.

At the outset, I mentioned a Christian woman struggling with pornography. In 2007 Nielsen//NetRatings found that approximately thirteen million American women click on pornographic sites each month, comprising roughly one in three visitors to adult entertainment websites. Pornography is not a man-only issue. *Fifty Shades of Grey*, marketed to women, was reported by *Business Insider* to be the fastest selling Kindle e-book and paperback novel in history. There is no wonder that many women picking up these books are also clicking on the screen.

It is a stereotype and a really, really, really bad rumor that women don't struggle with sexual sin—or so it appears. Most of the books, sermons, and articles addressing sexual temptation are geared towards men. There is no doubt that men need to hear these things, but so do women. The sin which corrupted all that was beautiful in the world also corrupted us women. I know that for many it is difficult to grasp; but remember, the Proverbs are filled with warnings about the adulterous woman. When great men fall it is not always because of sexual sin, but so often it is because of adultery. I am not saying it is the woman's fault. No way. It takes two to tango. But what I am saying is that all Scripture is useful, and therefore those texts aren't only meant for men; they are also meant to teach women and to warn us of the dangers of being that temptress, that adulterous woman. Don't forget to warn women as well as men about the dangers of sexual sin.

There are other issues regarding women and sexuality. Obviously, there is the issue of marriage and purity. There is the issue of the purity culture. There is the issue of fear and pressure because of the effects of pornography. There is abortion and, of course, same-sex attraction. Those are all issues that I did not address, but ones that merit discussion. This shouldn't be the end of the conversation, but it should be the beginning. There are two things that I want you to remember: There are some women who are *suffering*, and there are some women who are *struggling*—suffering because of the hands of another, and struggling with their own sin and temptation.

But not all is drab. The good news is there really is good news in the gospel. We know that the gospel transforms lives; the fall of man will not have the last word. Jesus' cross crushes the power of sin. We can resist temptation, and one day the Lord will make all things new. This is good news. One day we will again be naked and unashamed. Remember the story of my friend, the one who had the secret porn addiction? The apostle John tells us in I John 1:9, "If we confess our sins, he is faithful and just to forgive us our sins and cleanse us from all unrighteousness." The Lord is faithful to do what he says he will do. My friend confessed her sin, and the Lord was faithful to change her. He isn't finished with her or any of us. He promises to finish the good work he began, and he who calls us is faithful. He will surely do it.

REVIEW QUESTIONS

1. *What issues of sexual brokenness are especially difficult for women?*

2. *How can the church help women pursue holiness in their sexuality? How do we minister to those who are* suffering *and those who are* struggling? *How do we show them the love of Christ?*

≡ 9 ≡
TRAFFIC STOP:
HOW THE GOSPEL CAN
OVERCOME SEX TRAFFICKING

TONY MERIDA

Today, I hope to give you some biblical and practical things that we can do to combat the issue of sex trafficking.

Most conservative types that I meet don't have a problem with us engaging in combating this issue. Most people would not say, "We shouldn't fight against sex trafficking." It's almost like saying you hate orphans. No one would say that except the guy on *Nacho Libre*, who in that great theological movie declared, "I hate all the orphans in the world!" Most people would not say that about sex trafficking. But I do often hear from conservative evangelicals a strange cynicism about this issue in a variety of ways. I hear, "You guys talk about fighting trafficking, but you don't talk about fighting abortion." They claim, "You talk about sex trafficking, but you're not standing up for the marriage issue." I get a bit bothered by this coldwater committee. They have made these comments because they assume people aren't doing all of these things, that we are just picking one or the other. I could rattle off a list of people who are trying to take the whole of the Bible and work it out practically. I think a lot of these comments are smoke screens or attempts to justify ourselves for why we are not doing anything personally.

Others talk about sex trafficking as a purely international problem. They don't realize sex trafficking is happening in their own hometown. If Satan is active in your town and if you are in a sexualized culture, then you have sex trafficking in your town.

Many also overestimate what is actually being done. Many people aren't getting involved because they think others have addressed the issue. For example, they think that because the Passion movement took up an offering and people stamped their hands and said, "End it," that we are actually making progress. In reality, this is a massive mountain that needs to be melted and will take years to combat. We shouldn't interpret certain testimonies as great, massive victories. We should celebrate the victories—and there are victories out there that should give us hope as we combat this problem—but don't overestimate what's going on. This is the second largest, and the fastest growing, criminal enterprise in the world. Stamping our hands doesn't mean we are really making a major impact.

I would like to raise three questions. First of all, why should I care about this problem? Secondly, what is the nature and scope of the problem? And thirdly, what are some biblical and practical things I can do about the problem, particularly in a way that would reflect the gospel?

Why should I care about the problem? I'm not a guru on this subject. I am an ordinary pastor. I teach at a seminary, but I don't even teach this subject. Why do I care about sex trafficking? Two reasons: I care about the Bible, and I am a father. The first one is sufficient. You don't have to be a parent to care about fighting sex trafficking, but it is worth mentioning. I care about fighting this issue because I care about Scripture. I'm not into justice because it's cool. I'm into justice because it's in the Bible.

About six years ago, I was asked by a Southern Baptist youth camp to do a bible study on the poor. I thought it would be an easy week of camp: I'll talk about the poor, I'll tell some stories. I don't know what kind of impact the week made upon the students and the adults, but it really wrecked my own life. I began to read the Bible, putting aside any preconceptions as best I could, to see what it says about the poor. I began to see the trio of the vulnerable—the orphan, the widow, and the sojourner—continue to pop up. I continued to read passages about God's own character, about his justice. As I was teaching these kids and adults about our need to do Micah 6:8—to do justice and love mercy and walk humbly with our God—I got convicted by my own preaching. It's a miserable place to be to be preaching to people while knowing that you need to repent. So, I repented of my inactivity and my sin of omission, my sin of doing absolutely nothing. I came across quotes like this one by Martin Luther King, Jr., who said, "He who passively accepts evil is as much involved in it as he who helps to perpetuate it." I became aware that I had adopted a standard of spiritual maturity that basically measured my life against my peers, rather than trying to conform the whole of my life to the whole of the Bible. When I tried to conform the whole of my life to the whole of the Bible, there were some very obvious deficiencies.

This led my wife and me into an unfamiliar world of ministry. We ended up adopting five children—four from Ukraine and one from Ethiopia. We began to do work fighting injustice. My wife now serves as a volunteer representative for International Justice Mission, which is involved not just with sex trafficking, but with everything from land grabbing to other forms of slavery. We reoriented our lives. We began to attend entirely different conferences. We planted a church that included a concern for the orphan and the oppressed as part of its global missions strategy. Please understand I am not trying to commend my way of life as a standard for anyone to follow. I share it to encourage you personally as you are teaching others to conform their lives to Scripture. We are all going to apply this differently based on our age and our experience.

The Bible drove William Wilberforce. He was not a political pragmatist. He was a radically God-centered Christian who was a politician, and his true affections for God, based on the "peculiar doctrines of Christianity" (as Wilberforce called them), were the roots of his endurance for the cause of justice. These peculiar doctrines found in the Scriptures became the source of motivation and endurance for Wilberforce.[1]

A few biblical doctrines changed our lives. One of them was simply the concept of biblical justice. You begin to see it as you read through the Bible. In our church, we typically preach through books of the Bible, and we recently went through the books of I and II Kings. Throughout those books, kings were called to rule with wisdom and with justice. We see this through the book of Proverbs, as well. Unfortunately, as you know, all the kings failed, but Jesus is the king to end all kings, and he came and ruled with justice. In his second coming, he will rule with total, perfect justice. We began to see this and read verses like Psalm 99:4, "The king in his might loves justice." God loves it. The king loves it. We began to read passages like Matthew 23:23 when Jesus said, "Woe to you, scribes and Pharisees, hypocrites! For you tithe mint and dill and cumin, and have neglected the weightier matters of the law: justice and mercy and faithfulness." That's what I felt like in my life. I had neglected weightier matters of justice and mercy and faithfulness. Spurgeon has an awesome sermon that you can find online called "The Lord's Famous Titles," in which he goes through the titles of God from Psalm 146. The sermon

1   See John Piper, *Amazing Grace in the Life of William Wilberforce* (Wheaton, Ill.: Crossway, 2007).

describes how God executes justice for the oppressed, how he's a father to the fatherless, and so on. Of course, Micah 6:8, which many have referred to as a one-line summary of the whole law, is foundational for biblical justice.

I had read these verses before. I went to seminary. I just had many excuses not to take them at face value. I thought, "Liberal theologians do social justice; I don't want to go down that slippery slope." At this point, I have heard the slippery slope argument about all I can take. It just doesn't work. It's not an argument. If you follow this logic, you wouldn't do anything, including eating tonight because you might eat too much. You don't want to go down that slippery slope. I had this reservation: That's fine for some people to do, but that is not at the heart of what it means to follow Jesus. To which I now ask: Is Jesus not living out Micah 6:8 perfectly? Is following Jesus not about living like him? Is he not loving God and neighbor perfectly? How could we say this is not part of what it means to follow Jesus? John Stott asked the question: What sort of person do we think Jesus Christ is? In John 11, he first snorted with anger in the face of death and then wept over the bereaved. If only we could be like Jesus, Stott says, indignant toward evil and compassionate toward its victims.[2] That's what I want to be like—indignant toward evil and compassionate toward its victims.

---

2 John R. W. Stott, *The Cross of Christ* (Downers Grove, Ill.: InterVarsity Press, 1986).

I had many other obstacles. I won't share all of them here. This is not personal therapy for Tony. However, you are going to hear them in conservative evangelicalism. Some will say, "That's the Old Testament; it was a theocracy." God's law is based on God's character. God's character has never changed. It never will change. You get the most pushback when you are talking about justice, especially if you look like me. I've heard, "Chris Daughtry is up there talking about social justice. He's a liberal, right? We are about evangelism, not social justice." Let me be very clear. I think we have to overemphasize evangelism. Justice is not evangelism. Justice should never replace evangelism. I love evangelism, but this excuse is filled with all sorts of problems and misconceptions. I have a suspicion that a lot of people, who say we should do evangelism, not justice, aren't doing either one, and they have never really attempted justice or mercy. In my brief five- or six-year journey of trying to serve in these areas, I have been able to talk to people about the gospel in places that I would have never been had I not gone there to do mercy and justice. If anything, I share the gospel more now because justice ministry takes me to the darkest places in the world, and in many cases, the least evangelized places in the world are where injustice reigns. We need to quit this silly argument and pray that God would simply give us a hearts of love for people. That's what we need. We need to stop with the arguments, and we need to say, "God, help us to love people." We don't make this argument with anything else.

We don't say, "You shouldn't vote, you should do evangelism. You shouldn't discipline your kids, you should be doing evangelism. You shouldn't have a quiet time, you should be doing evangelism." So why are we making it with this particular issue? I think it's because of our history. We should learn from history, but we should not be afraid of doing what the Bible tells us to do. Loving our neighbor is never a move in the wrong direction.

We often miss this concept of biblical justice because we live in a nation where the rule of law is expected. If you lived in a country where injustice reigns, one of the first features of God's nature that would draw you is his justice, how God is on the side of the oppressed. A couple of years ago, my kids were out riding their bikes in the street in our neighborhood and this car zoomed past at about sixty miles-an-hour. When the driver came back and did it again, I took a picture of his car. I ran up to our bedroom to get the phone, and my wife had already called the police, which was what I was about to do. The police came, stopped this individual, and justice was served while we sat on our front porch, thrilled. That doesn't happen everywhere. We take this for granted.

Christopher J. H. Wright told a story about a kid from India that grew up in a very poor, oppressed village. His family had been exploited and abused for years, and he grew up with a great sense of wanting to correct this oppression. He ran into a group of Christians who gave him a Bible. For whatever reason, the first story this Indian kid read was the story of Naboth's vineyard and King Ahab, who was called the "vile human toad who squatted on the throne of Israel" by the old famous Southern Baptist, R. G. Lee. Ahab had everything else, but he wanted Naboth's vineyard. His wicked wife, Jezebel, put a plan together to kill Naboth. An innocent man died and no one in the city did anything. But God was aware of it. Elijah comes, sticks his finger in Ahab's face, and God executes justice. The Indian kid who read this story was so drawn to a God who cares for the oppressed that he began to read story after story. We take this attribute of God for granted because our nation is founded on justice and liberty. In many places of the world, it's not. It's absent. We miss this very attractive attribute because of our own context.

Another concept of justice in the kingdom of God that really impacted me was an already-but-not-yet vision of the kingdom. Not yet do we see perfect justice, but we will. Total *shalom* will reign; the lion and the lamb will play together. There is no more trafficking; there are no more orphans. There is no Russia, no Ukraine, and no United States. There is only a kingdom and a king with scars in his hands. We long for that not-yet day. Right now, when we do justice it gives people a taste of what is coming. We get to bear witness of what the kingdom of God is like, what our king is like and, if you like, bring the future into the present by everyday acts of justice and mercy.

These biblical convictions really compelled me. I began to see how God set up laws in the Old Testament to protect the abused and how God's plan has always been for his people to step up, to shine a light in dark places. So, one reason why I care about justice is because I care about the Bible.

Secondly, I care about justice because I have three daughters from Eastern Europe. One of the reasons I am a proponent of international adoption is that a very high percentage of those children who aren't adopted end up in a life of prostitution, trafficking, and crime. Upwards of 80 percent of the girls who don't get adopted in Ukraine end up in prostitution. Since 1991, Americans have adopted over 60,000 children from Russia, though now adoption in that country is significantly restricted. Today in Crimea—Crimea is now under the control of Russia—there are 4,300 orphans languishing in an orphanage. We don't see them on the news. We don't hear their stories because they are voiceless. They are powerless.

Thinking about these girls, who could be your daughters, being trafficked should end all discussion as to whether or not we should do it. One of the reasons I love Liam Neeson's movie *Taken* is because I'd like to be him. In the movie, his daughter goes on a trip to Paris, and a ring of traffickers takes her and her friend. But they kidnap the wrong girl. Liam Neeson says: I don't have any money, but I have a certain set of skills I have acquired over a lifetime, and I will find you. He does, and it is awesome. Sadly, we aren't Liam Neeson. He trained Batman. We won't compare to Liam Neeson. He fights wolves with his bare hands in one movie. He's Aslan, for goodness sake. We are not Liam Neeson. We are going to have to have a different plan than that, though we admire that.

My friend David Platt tells of a trip he made to Nepal. He was walking through this impoverished village and had been instructed not to give anyone any food because of the dependency it created and because the workers there had a plan to take care of the village. The whole time, this one girl kept pulling on his arm and asking him for food. She was so malnourished. David said she eventually got so mad that he wouldn't give her any food that she tried to spit at him, but she didn't have any saliva. He said he had this thought: What would I do if this were my daughter? It's a good question on this issue. We wouldn't have silly arguments as to whether or not we should do this. We would do everything we could to help.

So, question one: why should I care? I care because I believe the Bible and am a parent.

Question two: what is the nature and scope of the problem? At a very street-level definition, sex trafficking is rape for profit. It involves deception, coercion, and force. Traffickers transport victims for the purpose of sexual exploitation. It often thrives in areas that lack robust law enforcement. Gary Haugen's important book, *The Locust Effect*, contends that to end the war on trafficking you have to end the war on violence. We have to establish the rule of law to have sustainable justice in particular areas.

Here are some of the facts about trafficking. It is the second largest criminal industry in the world and the fastest growing.

There are two million children, according to UNICEF, in the commercial sex trade—two million children. Eighty percent of the victims are women, and up to 50 percent are minors. The total market value of elicit human trafficking is estimated at over thirty-two billion dollars. It is an engine of the global AIDS epidemic.

How does it happen? People prey on the vulnerable. Let me give you a few cases of how this sort of thing happens:

A fourteen-year-old runs away from her abusive home. She meets a woman who offers her a job selling fabric. The next day she wakes up in a brothel.

Kim's first abuser was when she was thirteen-year-old. It was her father, followed by her brother, two of her mother's boyfriends, and then a stepfather. She ran away from home, from all of this, when she was thirteen to live with her eighteen-year-old boyfriend, who groomed her to be a prostitute through his friends. He abused her and sold her to another pimp when she was fourteen years old.

Locally, this happens in all sorts of ways. My wife was talking to a lady in Raleigh, who at eighteen-months-old was sold by her parents, who were part of a satanic cult that abused children. She was abused from house to house all throughout her childhood. In our town, a lady sold her three-year-old for drugs.

Internationally, victimization often happens through false promises. A fourteen-year-old is told that she can leave her poor, abusive home and come to the United States for an education and a job. She comes and is taken, hooked on drugs, and sold. In many impoverished countries, sadly, families give up their children. Miriam, a Kazakh girl, was sold for three hundred dollars to a man from Russia who promised to put her to work as a shop assistant. When she arrived in Russia, she found that her new home was a barred cell with a locked metal door. Jenny, a fourteen-year-old Nigerian girl, was sold to a married couple in the United States as a nanny for their children. For five years she was raped by her employer and abused by his wife.

Atlanta is the number one place in the United States for sex trafficking. Many refer to Atlanta as "sex city." This is due to all the large interstates that pass through there, the conventions that are held there, and the world's busiest airport. One writer says that instead of traveling to Thailand to have sex with a child, men are now traveling to Atlanta. A pimp picks them up at Hartsfield–Jackson International Airport and takes them to have sex with a child sex slave. He then drops the men off at the airport to fly home for dinner with their families the same night. These men aren't all internationals. Today, when you go to Atlanta's airport, there will be signs at counters: If you know someone who is being trafficked or if you are, here's who to call.

My wife and I spent a short time in Hattiesburg, Mississippi. We were coming out of a pizza joint when we noticed a hair and nail salon filled with young Asian girls working. An older guy with gray hair came out and got into his big pickup truck. He just looked suspicious. We called a friend that works with an anti-trafficking organization, and he verified that this particular place was raided just a few weeks earlier for prostitution—in Hattiesburg, Mississippi.

One of the saddest cases in Raleigh-Durham, where I live now, happened not long ago. A fifty-year-old single lady ended up with five children in her home when her daughter went to prison. Unfortunately, she had no diploma, no GED, and was extremely limited on where she could work. She went to work for a local food chain that is on every corner, trying to provide for these five little kids, one of whom was nursing. At the establishment she was abused. The abuse went from verbal to physical to sexual by her boss. Then her boss began to sell her to employees. She threatened to call the police. He informed her that if she did, she wouldn't have a job, and no one else would hire her. How else would she provide for these five kids, he said. When she did turn him in, the police officer joined in the party and became a perpetuator himself. She was trapped; she was exploited. She was victimized. Eventually she got free, got rehab, vocational training, a GED, and a new job. This doesn't just happen in Cambodia and Vietnam. This is everywhere.

How can we respond biblically and practically to the problem of sex trafficking? The book of Ephesians provides four challenges for what we can do as evangelicals who love the gospel, love people, and want to follow Jesus and flood the darkness with light. The Bible is not foreign to this sort of reality. The Bible is a realistic book. We have statements in the book of Ephesians about this sort of darkness. In Ephesians, the fifth chapter in particular, Paul talks about this theme of darkness and light.

The city of Ephesus was very similar to the world just described, although it's hard to imagine anything darker. Ephesus was a port city and a gateway to Asia. Today, if you visit the ruins of ancient Ephesus, you can still see an inscription giving directions to the brothels. That's the situation Paul is writing about in the book of Ephesians. He mentions these "formerly, but now" statements in chapters 1 and 2. Formerly you were this, but now you are this. He gives this beautiful picture of it in chapter 5 when he says, "You were darkness; now you are light."

When we look at the book of Ephesians, we are reminded that in the middle of all this darkness were the saints. In the middle of the darkness was this little colony of the kingdom, this little outpost that was to shine the light of truth and love to a sex-filled culture. While Paul doesn't mention sex trafficking in chapter 5, he does speak in ways that connect to sex trafficking. For example, in Ephesians 5:3 he says, "But sexual immorality and all impurity or covetousness must not even be named among you." In Greek, *porneia* refers to sexual immorality or impurity. Verse 5 includes "everyone who is sexually immoral or impure, or who is covetous." I am sure Paul would have been okay with applying this to those in the brothels and he would be okay with us applying it to sex trafficking. If verse 12 doesn't nail sex trafficking, I don't know what does. It says, "For it is shameful even to speak of the things that they do in secret." Paul tells us what we ought to be doing positively when he says in verse 13, "But when anything is exposed by the light, it becomes visible," and also in verse 11, "Take no part in the unfruitful works of darkness, but instead expose them."

This passage is a description of a dark, sex-driven culture and of how the saints are to live in a twisted and corrupt culture. This darkness is described in Romans 1, working itself out in all types of sins. Romans 1:21 says, "Their senseless minds were darkened." Paul lists things that relate to trafficking, like deceit, malice, and haughtiness. In Romans 1, he calls these individuals "inventors of evil."

Our first challenge as God's people who walk in the light is to end—and we need to encourage our people to end—our involvement with every form of *porneia*. As Ephesians 5:3 says, there shouldn't be a hint of it. Verse 6 the wrath of God is coming because of sins like it. Verse 7 don't associate with people in it. Verse 8—become who you are. First, if you want to help fight sex trafficking, stop looking at porn. I don't think people make this connection. The eighteen-month-old baby who is sold, the girl who is trafficked at the Atlanta airport, and your pornography addiction are related. You can have a college student, for example—I'll pick on them who has "End It" stamps, wants to fight sex trafficking, but has a pornography addiction. There is a massive disconnect there. Pornography is creating the demand for sex trafficking, and in many ways, it's a gateway drug to sex trafficking. I believe if you are looking at pornography, you are perpetuating the problem of sex trafficking. You are involved in sex trafficking. Do you realize what you are perpetuating by indulging in this? Many of the ladies that men, and also women, view are victims of sex trafficking. Martin Luther King, Jr., says, "Darkness cannot drive out darkness: only light can do that." You want to affect the dark world of trafficking? You need to walk in light. We need to tell our friends, and we need to tell our churches, to end every involvement they have with *porneia*.

Secondly, endeavor by God's power to live a life of goodness, righteousness, and truth. Live an everyday life of justice. Paul says, "For you were once darkness, but now you are light in the Lord. Walk as children of light—for the fruit of the light results in all goodness, righteousness, and truth" (Eph 5:8–9). In these trio of terms Paul almost summarizes Christian ethics. All that is good and right and true is what the Christian is to be about. We don't simply go do justice; we live a life of justice. We don't simply do good; we live a life of goodness. Out of lives of holiness and justice and goodness and truth, we affect darkness. In all of our dealings with people, we should pursue justice.

I love the concept that Job expresses in Job 29 when he says, "I put on righteousness and it clothed me. My justice was like a robe and a turban." He says: I wear justice. I put on justice like you put on clothes. I live with a social conscience. I live every day of my life looking out for the oppressed, looking out for the vulnerable, looking to be honest in all of my dealings. We should put justice on every day. Use your gifts. Use your abilities. Use your rhythms. Use your vocation in a way that can make a difference. For example, you could contact lawmakers and advocate for this issue. You could become a lawyer devoted to prosecuting these cases, which the vulnerable all around the world desperately need. You could support local police enforcement. Business professionals could address issues of poverty, which often perpetuate the problem of sex trafficking, by doing business as mission. We could provide vocational training for people who are vulnerable. We could do foster care, which is another group of vulnerable people. We could provide basic hospitality for the snotty-nosed kid down the street whose dad is in jail and mom is on crack. We welcome them in because God knows what's going to happen to these individuals. Perpetrators prey on the vulnerable. We have to teach our people, that when it's in your power to do good, do it. When you take the opportunity to bless and to welcome and to care for the vulnerable, you are in many ways helping to prevent this massive problem of trafficking.

I believe churches need to consider developing aftercare facilities and ministries. It is one of the best ways we can minister in this world of sex trafficking. Not all of us can be lawyers or politicians, but when these girls are rescued, they need to see what a family looks like. They need the gospel. They need to come into a worshipping community and see what that's like. One of the most fruitful ministries our church has had came through locking arms with a rescue shelter. We were considered a safe church where these women could come and worship, and they would come every week. They spent time in my home. We would provide respite care by taking these individuals into our own home, so that those who work in these shelters could go out for a weekend. Be on guard. Be on the lookout for ways you could simply do basic goodness, righteousness, and truth.

In your own local church, please do background checks on volunteers and practice church discipline wisely and faithfully. Report suspected abuse to the proper authorities.

The National Human Trafficking Resource Center, which is managed by the Polaris Project in Washington, D.C., can be reached at (888) 373-7888. Use this number to report a tip. Give them a call or a text. You can connect with anti-trafficking services in your area with this number. You can request training with this number. I also encourage our students to do this.

When you travel to teach at a seminary or a church, teach about justice. We have to promote in-country adoption. We have to promote in-country justice work, because we aren't the saviors of the whole world. This work needs to be happening locally. We should promote simple expositional preaching and teaching that applies the truths of the Bible all over the world.

We need men, in particular, to serve. Men primarily cause the problem, and men are normally the last to help. There are exceptions, and we are grateful for the exceptions. But we need men. Men are often abusive or passive. They are bullies or cowards. It's the gospel that makes us humble and courageous. Those are the types of men we need, like Wilberforce—all five-foot-three of him—who for forty-six years worked to abolish slavery. He had a chance at one time to be the Prime Minister of England, and he said no because he wanted to free people who would never even say thank you. We need a generation of men like that.

Challenge three: expose the dark world of sex trafficking. Ephesians 5:11 says, "Take no part in unfruitful works of darkness, but instead expose them." Believers are to not participate in sexual sin, but we don't keep our light under a bushel. We flood the world with light, exposing the sin of unbelievers. This word "expose" in the Greek means to correct or convince. Paul does not tell us here how we ought to expose those shameful sins that people are doing in secret, but surely it means by our words and our deeds. This will be different for everyone. I follow the Good Samaritan principle on this. We can't do everything, but we can meet needs in our area. What can be done to expose the problem? How can you use words? How can you use your deeds? We will all answer this differently, but we can't live with our head in the sand. Perhaps you would form a justice team in your local church. Perhaps you would do a community assessment, a great tool provided by International Justice Mission, to evaluate your own context.[3] You could contact local services and ask how you can help them. Live your life with your eyes open.

---

3   Available at www.ijm.org/resources

Finally, number four, we need to evangelize those in darkness. Light not only exposes sin, but it transforms unbelievers into the realm of light. That is the beauty of the gospel. How does the gospel overcome sex trafficking? The gospel combats two of Satan's primary works. Satan is an accuser and a deceiver. The gospel brings truth that exposes this deception. God convicts us of sin—and that is God's love for us, that he would expose our sin and lead us to repentance. The gospel brings to bear truth that tells people, "You can't live under this deception. This is sin." The gospel works against the accusations of the devil, who tells these victims, "You are nothing." Many of these victims feel an enormous sense of shame and brokenness. The gospel says there is no condemnation for those who are in Christ Jesus and that we stand holy and blameless before him. Only the gospel brings that sense of wholeness. This gospel is the power of God unto salvation that can transform even the perpetrators' lives, who are, ironically, slaves themselves. We should go into this world of darkness, taking the light of the gospel that melts the mountains. Take the light of the gospel that exposes the deceit, and when deceit is exposed, bring the medicine of the gospel. J. B. Phillips translates verse 14 like this, "It's even possible (after all, it happened to you!) for light to turn the thing it shines upon into light also." When the gospel goes into dark places it can transform people into the realm of light.

Remember these few things when you think about evangelism. God transformed many in this Ephesian congregation who had come out of this lifestyle. This church was probably filled with those individuals. The gospel transformed Paul who wrote this letter. Some need to hear the gospel when they are freed. Some need to be freed in order to hear the gospel. I have seen both happen. I have seen a young girl, who had been taken by a gang in northern Virginia and sold, become a believer, and she was baptized gloriously. She was freed. She heard the gospel. She was really freed. Others can't hear the gospel until they are freed. You can draw a tight connection to the book of Exodus where God says: I want my people to go so that they may worship me—because it's hard to worship when you are carrying rocks all day in Egypt. It's hard to worship when you are so crushed with despair that you are just trying to survive. So often, you hear people say we should be about proclamation. I agree. Alleviating eternal suffering is primary to temporal suffering, but they can't hear our proclamation when they are on drugs and raped six times a day. For many of the two million underage people trapped in trafficking, we have to work to free them in order for them to hear the gospel.

We must pursue, as best as we can, an integrative model of mission that takes both physical and spiritual needs seriously. We want to alleviate temporal suffering, and we definitely want to alleviate eternal suffering. Jesus didn't wake up every day and ask, "Should I do justice or evangelism today?" No, Jesus went out and loved his neighbor, and that involved both—caring for the totality of a person.

Why should we care about this problem? If we care about the Bible, we are going to bump into this issue a lot. We all need to prayerfully apply the teaching of the Bible in areas that are uncomfortable for us, conforming our lives to the whole of the Bible. Secondly, what's the scope of it? This is the fastest growing crime in the world, and it is a world of demonic darkness, filled with the schemes of the devil. What are some ways we can respond? We need to end all involvement with *porneia*. We need to endeavor to live a life of goodness, righteousness, and truth. We need to expose the dark world of sex trafficking, and we need to evangelize those in the darkness.

May God by his grace help us to do these things as the children of light.

REVIEW QUESTIONS

1. *What were you surprised to learn about sex trafficking?*

2. *What does the Bible teach about the concept of justice? Why should Christians care about justice?*

3. *How can the church—and you personally—address issues of sex trafficking and other forms of exploitation?*

═ 10 ═

KEEPING THE MARRIAGE BED PURE: THE GOSPEL AND MARITAL SEXUALITY

KEVIN SMITH

Hebrews 13

Nothing has consumed the lives of my wife and me like laboring with couples in the churches that I have been blessed to serve. Nothing has been as heartbreaking for me as a pastor as dealing with various issues of marriage among families. Scripture affirms that marriage is God's institution, and I want to begin with the presupposition that marriage is good for everyone. Marriage is part of God's ordained order in creation. Many times in our culture, people try to describe certain things as good for you "church folk," but not necessarily good for anyone else. Based on the Word of God, I suggest that marriage is the good, profitable, and godly way for male and female to covenant in a relationship that will bring forth fruit for the propagation of humanity in ways that are prosperous and good, or as many would say, "flourishing."

I also want to suggest that God's Word is true, and if we were to examine the fruit of pursuing sexuality in ways other than God's Word, we would find such fruit is not good. I have not found any retired black grandmamma rejoicing at raising her grandkids because her son or her daughter is producing children outside of wedlock and not being responsible. No young lady in her late twenties, who has now decided to get married is happy that a certain intimacy in her marriage has been lost because of the trail of men that she slept with through high school and college. No man is happy to go back to his college reunion, walk around with his wife, and introduce her to the line of women he slept with throughout college in ungodly sexuality. I would be very happy to talk to people about the fruit, reality, and results of sexuality pursued outside of what God has ordained in creation for male and female created in his image and his likeness.

Hebrews 13: 4 says, "Marriage should be honored by all and the marriage bed kept pure. For God will judge the adulterer and all the sexually immoral." As we seek to keep the marriage bed pure and to honor God's Word, we must realize that the over-sexualization of our society can't lead to the a-sexualization of the church. As we reject and acknowledge the sinfulness, hurtfulness, and harmful results of the over-sexualization of our culture, we can't get to a place where the church does not talk about and teach about sex.

I wonder how many sermons have been preached within the last year addressing sex, adultery, or divorce. The Bible says that God will judge the adulterer, the sexually immoral. Those who ignore and reject God's ordained sexual pattern will endure consequences. Why? Because sexuality within the covenant of marriage is so important to God's ordained order. Sexuality in the covenant of marriage is the only pure way to pursue sexuality that will honor God and honor one another as male and female created in the image and likeness of God. Marriage is so important that God says he will deal with the sinfulness of those who pursue sexuality in ungodly manners. We should recover the terms of "ungodly," "unrighteous," and just "sin." Christians should clearly understand that legality does not determine whether a thing is good, profitable, and godly. I mean, it is not illegal to get drunk in your basement, but it is sin. And the children of the basement drunk will tell you it's unprofitable, and the wife or the husband of the basement drunk will tell you it ain't good. And so what is legal does not in any way determine what is good, profitable, and ultimately what is godly. The church must discuss sex. Even as we reject the over-sexualization of our culture, we must speak about sex in ways that have been revealed in the Word of God. We must discuss sex in ways that reflect God's glory, as men and women pursue their God-given sexual nature in a way that glorifies and honors God.

I certainly hope that as we teach what the Bible says about sexuality, we will keep the tone of the Scripture. Let us be clear, honest, and open as we teach the Word of God and address issues of sexuality among and outside of God's people. Certainly, let us avoid vulgarity and anything that would remove the mystery of sexual intimacy between husband and wife.

I am tired of preachers bragging about their "hot wife." Number one, "hot" is an objectifying term. There's nothing good, profitable, or godly about calling your wife hot in public. All it does really is set up an examination of your wife where someone says, "Oh, yeah, she *is* hot!" Now what fool wants somebody else to say that about his wife? Or what if someone says, "She ain't really all that hot?" As preachers, let's respect the tone, sensitivity, and mystique of sexuality as it is presented in the Scriptures and not use objectifying language that comes from movies and music videos.

Furthermore, the cultural practice of "flattening" sex to merely physical engagement and mechanics removes its emotional, commitment, and intellectual content; it removes many aspects of the one-flesh union expressed in Scripture; and ultimately it removes what we understand from Ephesians 5 to be the picture of the relationship between Christ and his church. When we proclaim the Word of God and speak of sexuality in a biblical context, we heighten the conversation. Scripture does not make sex less dramatic; the biblical context makes sex more dramatic. Sex is not only physical, it is emotional and spiritual, and ultimately it points to the glory of God. Scripture proclaims the value of sex between a husband and a wife in the covenant of marriage; let us speak of these things in a way that is influenced by Scripture.

The marriage bed is honorable for all. Although the writer of Hebrews is addressing this letter to the Hebrews, he says here in the thirteenth chapter that marriage is honorable and good for all. In Genesis 2, marriage is ordained in creation as the good union that God has established for one man and for one woman, and it's good for all. It's not just good for Abraham and his descendents; it's not just good for Moses and those who have received the law on Mt. Sinai. No, no, no. Before the fall, before the choosing of Abraham, before the giving of the Law of Moses, God ordained that marriage is good and honorable among male and female, who are created in his image and his likeness. We must speak in those types of categories when we speak about marriage.

Culturally, we believe that marriage is good for all. Truth be told, sociologists, researchers, political scientists, and anthropologists alike believe marriage is good for all, because statistics support the statement. Consider the societal ills that result when men and women pursue sexuality outside of biblical bounds. Who looks at the rate of out-of-wedlock births among black people at the turn of the twentieth century when Jim Crow was in effect, and looks at the rate of black out-of-wedlock births now in 2014, how it has tripled, maybe even quadrupled, and proclaims the change a good thing? No one does that. And so, it is not that marriage is only good for church folk. Marriage is honorable and good for all who are created in the image and likeness of God. Marriage is good and honorable for all, and Scripture also says: let the marriage bed be pure or undefiled.

I have two main venues where I seek to be a witness for Christ and develop relationships. One is the venue of motorcycling and motorcycle rallies. In this venue and culture, there is a tremendous amount of brokenness, objectification, and victimization of women; dysfunctional family backgrounds; and a variety of things. The other area is among parents of children playing sports, as my children are active on such teams. I try to really invest in those relationships. It's amazing how much a person's worldview, or life patterns and schedules, revolve around sex or interaction with the opposite sex. Before I was a pastor, I was a chaplain in a county jail in Chattanooga, Tennessee. In my years as a chaplain, ninety-nine percent of the men came from fatherless situations. They came from very dysfunctional situations. In pastoral ministry, I meet people all the time who were bruised within their families of origin or by divorce. I am a child of divorce; my wife is a child of divorce.

Keeping the marriage bed pure, honoring God's design in marriage, and rebuilding and reestablishing a marriage culture among God's people are things we must do to counteract the fruits of years and years of biblical neglect among so-called believing Christians. The Bible clearly says that homosexuality is sin; there is no question about that. But I don't really have a lot of time to fight the "gay normalization agenda" people because the dysfunctional, bruised people I meet and pastor were not bruised by the homosexual normalization agenda. I encounter people who were bruised because their daddy left their mama for another woman. They were bruised because of the dysfunction that was going on in their heterosexual families. So I don't know what homosexuals shall do or can do to the institution of marriage in the future, but I know that marriage is jacked up right now in America in the popular culture and among believers because of heterosexuals. And that is where we need to strongly address some matters.

If you've never in twenty years said anything about divorce in the church culture, then shut up about gay marriage. You need to first fix some things in your own house before you be "Mr. Culture Warrior Man." And so we need to clear up some of these things that we have failed to address as so-called Bible-believing Christians.

One way couples neglect to keep the marriage bed pure is that once they become parents, they put the parenting role above their roles as husband and wife. I know a lot of couples who mainly parent their children, so conversations can become mostly about function and logistics. Let's coordinate our schedule for this week. Let's do this for this week. How are we going to do that? How are we going to do this? So when do you ever talk intimately?

A lot of times, parents totally lose the reality of being a husband and a wife. I do intense pastoral counseling with people who are getting used to being married and experiencing the struggles common to young couples. But the greatest, most intense pastoral counseling I do is when people begin to be empty nesters, because they have not nurtured their relationship as husband and wife. They have been parents together for eighteen or twenty years, but they have basically been roommates raising kids for eighteen or twenty years. Their bedroom is not a zone of privacy. Their bedroom doesn't say anything like "this is our space." Certainly, fathers, the Bible says raise your children in the fear and the admonition of the Lord. But certainly we should not make raising our kids such a dominant motif in our lives that we forget that we are husbands to our wives. The wife should not forget that she is a wife to her husband. Parenting trips up a lot of people when it comes to keeping the marriage bed pure; they don't pursue one another sexually and romantically. They don't engage one another. Encourage those you meet to avoid the parenting push-out.

Secondly, there is "Prudish Her" or "Puritan Him." These are people who love the Lord, but you'd find it hard to believe that they've ever read the book of Song of Solomon. These are the people I think Dr. Moore referenced as talking about sex as if talking about smoking. These are the people who consider sex a necessary evil. Prudish Her and Puritan Him need to examine all of Scripture and glory in the distinction that God designed between male and female, and they should see those interactions as positive and good. Teach your children the importance of intimacy between husbands and wives, and the need for parents to spend time apart from the children. We have almost become a youth dominated culture, and those who want to keep the marriage bed pure must regain the leadership of their family. Parents drive families, not children. So, the prudish wife needs to realize that femininity and the sexual distinction of a woman is a good thing. She needs to encourage herself and other young women to accent their femininity. The unisex push in our culture is a bad thing. I am discouraged when I've seen young girls come to youth group meetings in saggy jeans, boots, old sweatshirts, and baseball hats because they have not been taught to value a skirt. They have not been taught to value a dress. They have not been taught to value the things that distinguish women from men.

And then there's the puritanical husband. Some folks have recognized the over-sexualization and the sinfulness of sex in our culture, and have adopted a posture that is almost non-sexual or asexual. They pretend to not notice sexuality in women. We have got to lay out the biblical understanding of sexuality, the biblical understanding of male and female. I mean, the Bible not only mentions Rachel and Leah by name, but describes Rachel as fine! And Leah was alright. That's what the Word of God says. So, we can't become a Puritan Him or a Prudish Her that doesn't acknowledge the distinctions between male and female.

Thirdly, pornography, hard or soft, in video or literary forms, must be dealt with in order to keep the marriage bed pure.

In my experience as a pastor, I have never talked to a couple where one spouse was distressed about a lack of intimacy within their marriage, where the other spouse was not engaged in some type of pornography. Usually the spouse was pursuing sexual fulfillment in something outside the marriage, whether in romance novels or hardcore pornography. For the marriage bed to be pure, we must remember to avoid the things in our culture that would seek to elicit sexual satisfaction or fulfillment in anything or anyone other than our spouse. Any pursuit of sexual fulfillment outside the covenant of marriage between one husband and one wife is sin. Certainly you have read in the Bible where Jesus says that if you lust after a woman in your heart you have committed adultery with her. So, let's get above function and get to intentions, motivations, and thoughts. Our general culture is pornographic, inundated with "soft porn." When I'm watching sports with my kids, why does "she" need to tell me that it's good to buy a Volkswagen? One thing I want to encourage you to think about with couples in your church as you seek to provide pastoral leadership is the fact that sometimes men and women are not even cognizant of the ways in which they affect their spouse. I can't tell you how many guys go see movies with their wives and during the movie, their wives turn to them and ask, "Do you think she looks good?" I mean, that's one of those suicidal, stab-yourself-in-the-throat type questions. I mean, if the actress didn't look good, she wouldn't be in the movie. But when the wife asked to go to the movie, she wasn't thinking about the movie's pornographic soft content. She only considered the movie's positive reviews or popularity. We have to be more cognizant of what we are doing with popular entertainment because there is a soft pornography that pervades our culture, and it's so pervasive that we don't even notice it. We live in a cleavage-type culture. And the Bible says, "Rejoice in the breasts of your wife." It's kind of funny saying these kinds of things in the Southern Baptist Convention headquarters, but that's Scripture. We must understand that the over-sexualization of our culture is pulling people away from seeking sexual fulfillment within the covenant of marriage as God has ordained.

A fourth threat to the sanctity of the marriage bed is pulpit inadequacy. I teach Christian preaching at Southern Seminary in Louisville, and I certainly want to encourage preachers to be faithful to the proclamation of God's Word. There is no way you can preach the Bible and not address the things that the Bible addresses. Many men cannot have the confidence that Paul had when he said, "I have not shunned to preach unto you the whole counsel of God," because many men move around the Bible in a precarious manner seeking to preach the things that they want to preach. Preach the Word in season and out of season. A whole lot of what's going on in our church culture is laid at the feet of pulpit inadequacy.

I am an advocate for systematic teaching of the Word, book by book or chapter by chapter. In this manner, you will address the things that the Word of God addressed, rather than choosing a topic here or a topic there. Such a system allows you to preach through the Scriptures, whether you are preaching on divorce, sex, or marriage. However, if you do a topical series on sex, then there should be something going on to provoke you to do that; perhaps you are responding to a particular matter or trying to achieve a particular thing. Expositional, systematic preaching through the Scriptures provides the most natural platform to teach all that the Word of God teaches in its context and in the flow of Scripture, without a hit-and-miss style of picking topics and having people question your motive for a particular sermon.

Pulpit inadequacy rears its head when preachers avoid addressing what the Bible teaches. Hebrews 13:4 says that God will deal with fornicators and adulterers. And how many times does Jesus address the issue of divorce, how it leads to adultery and people becoming adulterers and adulteresses? And yet that is never mentioned in our pulpits. In many church traditions (not necessarily among Southern Baptists), I've seen a tradition of divorced pastors. I grew up in a church where the pastor was divorced. Well, certainly if the pastor is divorced, he won't clearly address the sinfulness and the harmful consequences of divorce. It's easy to scapegoat gay people. It's easy to scapegoat the culture war without proclaiming the Word of God to the people sitting in your congregations and looking in your face.

I am a complementarian. I believe, just as our *Baptist Faith and Message* says, that a pastor of a congregation should be a man according to the biblical principle of male leadership in the home and in the church. But getting women out of the pulpit is not a major agenda of mine, because even if all the women are removed, there will still be a lot of "girls" up there who are scared to stand flatfooted and proclaim what the Word of God says about divorce, adultery, remarriage, fornication, cohabitation, and a variety of heterosexual sins. Pulpit inadequacy has been significant for the last generation, and we need to reclaim the authority of God's Word in our proclamation.

A fifth concern of mine is poor Christology and a poor understanding of Genesis. If the Bible says, in Ephesians 5, that marriage reflects the relationship between Christ and his church, and if it tells husbands to love their wife as Christ loved the church and gave himself for her, then it is vital that husbands especially have a healthy, vital Christology and understanding of the person and work of Christ and his relationship to his church. It is vital that married couples have that understanding. Pulpit inadequacy not only yields poor preaching about sex, divorce, remarriage, and adultery, but also poor preaching about the person and the work of Jesus Christ. The generational effect of felt-needs preaching, that is, preaching what we think people want to hear and not exalting the unique work of Jesus Christ, has caused irreparable harm in the church world. With our understanding of Genesis, some Christians approach marriage like it is a purely Christian thing. No, marriage is good, profitable, and godly for the flourishing of humanity.

A sixth threat to the marriage bed is a perilous workplace. I want to encourage you to remind your church members and to counsel couples about some of the perilous challenges in the workplace. Most work settings—be they governmental, educational, or corporate—have no problem encouraging employees of the opposite sex to travel together. Most workplaces have no problem encouraging employees of the opposite sex to share an office. Many work settings have no recognition of the distinction between male and female and also some of the perilous interactions that can happen when you pair people together in close quarters for a long time. I like the fact that Proverbs uses the word "foolishness" for the rejection of God's word and God's truth, because some of the stuff we do in our culture is just foolish.

"Oh, my gosh!" they say. "We were just trying to be equal, and we put these few women on this submarine with a whole lot of men, and I just don't understand how these women come up pregnant!" Because you're a fool!

"Oh, my gosh! I just don't know how these female prison guards come up pregnant in an all male prison." Because you're a fool! You want to deny the distinction between male and female. You want to deny the inherent attractiveness between male and female which God has ordained, and then when you reap the consequences and havoc of ignoring the biblical truth of male and female, you wonder how certain things could happen. It can happen because we reject the truth of God's Word. Nothing is more important for the committed follower of Jesus Christ than to be in fellowship with God and to have the joy of the Holy Spirit. And so if a work setting needs to be adjusted, we need to do that. If another job needs to be sought, we need to do that. If we need to do things at our own expense to avoid awkward traveling arrangements, we need to do that. But believers need to have their eyes opened to the perilous nature of the workplace, which can affect keeping the marriage bed pure.

You don't like the Bible? You like sociology—give me some numbers. Ask your local sociologist about the number of affairs that begin in the workplace. You say, "I am empirical; I'm not spiritual." Okay, empirically ask your sociologists about the number of affairs that begin in the workplace. We need to avoid and be aware of the perilous workplace.

And finally, we need to embrace the pleasure principle. Growing up in Washington, D.C., I attended a Catholic school because the public schools were not in the best shape, and the Catholic schools were excellent. In that setting, I found that many people could garner a functional understanding of sex within the covenant context of marriage that was only linked to procreation, but never linked to a husband enjoying his wife and a wife enjoying her husband. We must recover the biblical understanding of pleasure in sexuality. Now, we don't need to recover it the way that some have sought to recover it by having beds on our pulpit and having your wife up there looking stupid. But we do need to recover an understanding that sex is pleasurable, and that pleasure is good and acceptable in the sight of God. Many times people accuse Christians of trying to hold people back from natural enjoyment and natural pleasure. Unfortunately, some uptight Christians are guilty of that charge. The pleasure principle is okay; just read the Song of Solomon. In Song of Solomon you clearly see the pleasure principle, but you also see the mysterious mystique about sexuality; it's not just all laid out there for public consumption. "Ain't my wife hot?"—That's such a clown thing to say, because you are broadcasting what God has provided for you. Let us pursue and present the pleasure principle in a biblically-based way.

Let us also say that those who reject godly sexuality miss out on the pleasure principle. Husbands and wives don't wake up with shame. Husbands and wives don't wake up having to sneak out of a certain place before a certain time of day to conceal their whereabouts. Husbands and wives do not have later regret. Husbands and wives pursue sexual intimacy with one another in the context of covenant marriage between one man and one woman, with the anointing of the Holy Ghost. Pursue sexuality such that you not only have personal power, but you have the power of the Holy Spirit flowing from God's pleasure with your actions.

That's how we keep the marriage bed pure. We remind believers that we are rooted in the created order of God, and God ordained sexual intimacy between one husband and one wife in the context of covenant marriage "till death do you part." This is the one-flesh union. We remind believers to make time for one another in marriage as they seek to rear their children. We remind Prudish Her and Puritan Him that sexuality is good, pleasant, pleasing, and pleasurable, as presented in God's Word. We warn ourselves and we warn other believers about the pornographic culture, both soft porn and hard porn.

We repent of pulpit inadequacy and poor preaching, and we train up preachers to proclaim the Word of God. We challenge pastors to open up the Word of God and teach the whole counsel of God. Jesus speaks to divorce and how it leads to adultery. We address poor Christology, our failed understanding of Genesis, and how marriage and sexuality are rooted in Scripture. We warn believers about the perilous workplaces in which they work, where the unisex push in our culture has tried to muffle the distinction between male and female. Yet when we get into these tight quarters, we still find there is a distinction and an attraction between male and female. Finally, we embrace the pleasure principle as we see in Song of Solomon and so many other places.

Remember the Genesis account of Adam having named the animals, which are then paired off after their kind. Adam is standing there like, "Man, I did what God told me to do. Everybody is paired off and all the animals are hooking up. I guess I'll just sit here." And God says it's not good for the man to be alone. And he brought the woman unto the man. He brought Eve unto Adam. And the Bible says that Adam said, "Whoooo! Now, we're talkin'!

Bone of my bones and flesh of my flesh! Now, we're talkin'!" We don't always capture in our English translations the excitement Adam felt at God's presentation of Eve.

We must recover God's understanding of sexual intimacy between one man and one woman in the covenant context of marriage.

Finally, let's remember these three words:

"Choosing." God the Father chose us in Christ Jesus before the foundation of the world. God chose Israel in the Old Testament as his covenant people. When a husband chooses a wife, and a wife chooses to accept the proposal of a husband, and they choose one another, God says that adultery and sexual immorality is a push against that choice, and he will not let that stand. That's why he said he will judge the adulterer and the sexually immoral. God chooses us. Let us remember that we choose our spouse, and we make covenant and commitment to them.

"Sacrifice." When the Bible says, "Husbands love your wives as Christ loved the church," let us remember the word "sacrifice." I am willing to serve and give myself for this person.

"Filling." And finally, in good Trinitarian form, God the Father chose God the Son; our Lord Jesus Christ was sacrificed on the cross for God's people; and finally on the day of Pentecost the worshippers were all filled with the Holy Spirit. Jesus says I will send you a comforter and he shall abide with you. Let us remember the word "filling." Let us remember the intimate unity between a husband and a wife, not only emotionally and intellectually, but also physically. That's why Paul says so many times in Corinthians, that sins within the body are of a different sort, for they create impressions that cannot be removed. We can be cleansed by the gospel. We can be forgiven in the gospel. We can receive restoration and reconciliation with God in the gospel, but we must tell our children and we must tell our teenagers that there are some things that you can lose in the physical body and never reclaim if you engage in sexuality outside of God's pattern. Let's remember those words as we keep the marriage bed pure.

May we press to keep the marriage bed pure among God's people, and may we press to declare the purity of marriage as created by God for all humanity. On those two fronts, may we keep the marriage bed pure in our culture.

REVIEW QUESTIONS

1. *How can a couple with children avoid neglecting their relationship as husband and wife?*

2. *How should Christians embrace the distinctions that God has designed between men and women?*

3. *How can Christians maintain purity in a culture filled with "soft pornography"?*

**LELAND
HOUSE**
PRESS

Leland House Press is a new initiative from The Ethics and Religious Liberty Commission. Leland House Press exists to equip and educate the local church about ethical and religious liberty issues through the publication of various eBooks and booklets.

For more information about Leland House Press and the latest titles, visit **erlc.com/leland**

Made in the USA
San Bernardino, CA
03 September 2015